SCIENCE WITH YOUNG CHILDREN

Bess-Gene Holt

SCIENCE
WITH
YOUNG
CHILDREN

Bess-Gene Holt

National Association for the Education of Young Children
Washington, D.C.

Photo credits

Cover: Stephen H. Saperstone
Ann-Marie Mott: 112
Joani Bogdanowicz: 105
Ellen Levine Ebert: 55, 87
Charles N. Estes: 33
Sandy Felsenthal: 50
Mary K. Gallagher: 68
John T. Harlan: 44
John G. Holt: 45
Jean-Claude Lejeune: 71
Ann-Marie Mott: 24, 64, 92, 113
National Instructional Television Center: 101

Library of Congress Catalog Card Number: 77-76828
ISBN Catalog Number: 0-912674-53-9
Printed in the United States of America.

CONTENTS

PREFACE

This book is intended primarily for persons who work directly with young children—parents and teachers. I have tried to stay within the realm of settings in and around homes and early childhood centers in the United States and Canada.

In teaching, knowledge of both what and how you are doing is important. If science awareness is yours, you will never be caught with nothing to do with children. Science is all around us, wherever we are. Thus, this book is designed to help both children and adults develop conceptualizations about science for a changing world and new children.

A further intent of this book is to keep the individual child in focus and intact despite the literary difficulties with nonsexist pronoun use in the singular form. I will use a few extra words to establish "her" or "him" as equally unique.

Some of this material was developed in response to a very special assignment, working with the Enabler Model sponsored by Planned Variation. I acknowledge with thanks the Office of Child Development's sponsorship and the help of the Head Start families and staff persons who enabled the Enabler.

The scientific advice of my husband, John, a microbiologist, has been great. His personal support has been magnificent. My daughters Susan, Eva, and Reenee gave ideas freely, and, having participated in these activities long before memory serves, helped more than they know. Thank you, family.

Bess-Gene Holt
Ames, Iowa
March 1977

vii

1

SCIENCE EDUCATION IN EARLY CHILDHOOD

If a child is to keep alive his inborn sense of wonder . . . he needs the companionship of at least one adult who can share it, rediscovering with him the joy, excitement and mystery of the world we live in. (Carson 1965, p. 45)

What you wonder about is what you know—as well as the other way around. With young children, science is continuous wondering, finding out, knowing. Science is thinking and doing and making the two go together. The raw materials and events of science are all around, at home, in the yard, and in early childhood and primary centers and schools. Science for young children is catching an insect in a jar, watching it, and feeling the importance of letting it go. It is playing in dishwater with a measuring cup. It is wearing a coat in winter and considering why it is warmer that way. It is seeing how crabs and spiders are alike. Most children discover the materials skillfully. Most are delighted participants in the events. Making a *science* experience out of a find or happening may require the sensitivity and hard work of an adult.

YOU ARE IMPORTANT

"At least one adult . . ."—you. You are parents. You are child care workers. You are students. You are professors. You and I are all the grown-up persons who willingly accept responsibility for the education of young children. You become and you are teachers. You are important because you are yourselves and because you extend yourselves to add enrichment, knowledge, and strength to the lives of children. You probably use and keep in mind a curriculum, some account of the experiences you want children to have for reasons you may or may not write down as educational goals, objectives, or outcomes. Almost all of you will include some specified aims concerning science education. I agree with you. Science should be well represented in your planning. I join you in sharing here some ways of doing so.

You include science because your experience—education, culture, and maturity—tells you that children benefit by knowing the causes of and reasons for things that happen in the world. You know they need to be able to seek answers and make sense out of what they find. You hope they also enjoy the phenomena—the objects, events, and relationships—of the world. You hope the mystery of possible truth just ahead brings excitement. You hope that wonderment feels good. Your part in all these science doings, learnings, and feelings is potent. Science education, like any other education, is at its best when it is individualized—that is, when you make it personal, well-matched with a child's unique learning style and interests, and when it is developmentally appropriate for a particular child's growing abilities. This means a lot of your energy has to go into planning it and setting it up to happen that way for each child.

It is the early childhood teacher's challenge to fit the truth of the world into the child's system of knowing it. I am assuming you have already taken on this challenge.

CHILDREN ARE IMPORTANT

Herbert Zim once said, "Young children are more scientists than they are anything else." Children bring many attributes to science experiences.

Children Are Talented

Children have abundant curiosity. Most are eager to explore, discover, learn, and create anew. Their active bodies propel them into experience. Generally, children are alert to movement, sensitive to changes, interested in variety and new things—some novelty as long as it is not overwhelming. They are keenly aware of what is going on in their immediate environments. If these sensitivities are not apparent, good teachers usually consider the first job is to bring them out, or about. Sometimes events in the province of science can help with that task, too.

Children Are Individuals

Each individual child will already have developed some selective focus or interests. She or he will seek certain kinds of experience and ignore the possibilities for other kinds. He or she will be using an individual way of seeking. Some children plunge into whatever is the loudest and fastest action available. Some will try the activity only later, after others have gone, or after others have been observed doing it. As a first reaction, some children touch, some smell, some ask questions of the teacher, some hide. A child is in the process of developing a preferred style of gathering, storing, and using information or of turning it off and tuning it out. Each child arrives at an event with her or his own set of expectations, learned through prior experiences. New experiences fit into a person's system *in that person's way.* Each child has individual ways of learning through experience.

Children Are Learners

One way to provide personal learning experiences for each individual is to start with the presumption that a child's own being is referent, baseline, and focal point. Children experience phenomena in relation to themselves. When two-year-old Stephanie learns "warm," it means warmer than her body feels. Stephanie's bathwater is warm to her touch; the October sun makes her cheek warm; the dog's fur warms her bare feet. Temperature measurement, later, will be Celsius, or maybe still Fahrenheit, but first of all it is pure Stephanie.

The greatest sources of early learning experiences are those closest to the child, of the child's own making, and directly related to her or his own self.

Later on, I suggest some reorganization of science curriculum thinking based on this concept. A closely related idea is that learning experiences be planned to expand gradually along increasingly distant dimensions radiating from the child's own self, immediate experiences, and developmental level.

Children Do

Another avenue to encourage personal learning is to involve each child directly, actively, and immediately upon noting that child's interest. Children appear to learn well what they do. Their physical contact with materials is a key. This means they touch the guinea pig. They work the pulley. Wondering and finding out means intense involvement in both doing and caring about phenomena of the world. The most successful—that is, remembered, handy, and useful—learning comes through direct participation, especially for young children.

"Young" children are specified, since the primary interest here is basic science experiences for children before they are nine years old. Young children *are* participators. Donald Neumann emphasizes "sciencing" activities for this personalized involvement.

> Basically, children who are engaged in sciencing are given a chance to observe and manipulate a variety of man-made and natural objects in ways that help them to recognize similarities, differences, and relationships among the objects and phenomena. They sniff, look at, listen to, feel, pinch and if possible taste a variety of materials in order to develop and extend their ability to make careful and accurate observations. (Neumann 1972, pp. 137-138)

Children Are Sensitive and Sensory

Children experience through *all* their senses, not only vision, hearing, touch, taste, and smell, but also kinesthetic sensing within the body. Feelings through which children experience also include sensations such as hunger, thirst, pain or aching, posture, balance, and sensing environmental temperature and the passage of diurnal (day-night) time.

People figured out the importance of perception a long time ago. Sensory training has been a thrust of early childhood education for several hundred years. Sensory training has double meaning when we talk about science because children find out about their world through their senses, each mode making its own contribution. In addition, understanding one's own sensory mechanisms and expanding sense capabilities for awareness and alertness is part of science education.

For example, four-year-old Christopher is listening to the radio. Maybe what he hears is louder than the radiator's hiss but softer than the diesel locomotive passing on the tracks outside. Maybe he hears a message; maybe he moves to the music; maybe he is annoyed or hurt by the static. He learns about sounds as he hears. Chris can also learn about listening. How does the radio sound when he puts his hands over his ears? When he taps his ears lightly with his palms? What happens when he uncovers his ears and opens his mouth

wide, wider? If Chris turns his head first to one side, then the other, turns his
back to the radio, then what? Chris is learning about how ears work with the rest of his body. He can learn how he can change sounds. He may want to put his ear over an empty paper cup or a glass, or both, and hear what happens to the sounds. He may put the cup on the radio, to the wall, or on a table and listen into it and from it. He may try listening through a long tube such as a paper roll. This may be the time to listen to the big conch shell whisper and discover that it is channeled sound—not "the sea"—that is the mystery. Would he also be learning something about the radio? Of course. You do not need to be an electronics expert to encourage him to get a lot out of listening.

SCIENCE IS IMPORTANT

This book is about teachers and children doing science. You are important. Children are important. Science is important. Science for young children has traditionally included experience with plants and gardening, animals, human growth, rocks, soil, weather, air, water, food chemistry, color phenomena, mirrors, magnets, and machines. We think basic science knowledge about ourselves and the world around us contributes greatly to the development of reasoning and reasonable human beings. These learnings may also help us stay alive; survival is most certainly a basic condition of growth.

Why plan science into the early childhood curriculum? For one thing, it is entirely appropriate. The study of the phenomena of the world is exactly compatible with the nature of children. That is not so strange. Children are phenomena of the world, and natural ones at that. Scientifically speaking, humans are very much a part of the natural world; we affect the rest of the world and vice versa. We are a part of the scheme. We do not have a scheme all to ourselves or a separate set of rules. The current picture of the relations among objects, resources, and various forms of life, suggests some necessary and immediate additions to the traditions of science education. I think children may need to know more, and I feel strongly that they need to know some things differently. The attitudes toward the world and one's place within it form in the early years.

Healthy self-concept development can find strong support in the sharing of a reverence for life—all life. Children who appreciate and celebrate life have a healthy self-concept without the need to feel superior. Science is first of all a quest for understanding of our own beings, of nature and our own part in it, and of natural change, which includes growth of each child.

Learning the limits of knowledge is an important facet of science, too, perhaps now more than ever. Children should find out not only their own limitations, but those of any and all adults. Scientists do not know everything. They cannot solve all problems.

The contributions of science experiences to the intellectual development of children has been emphasized for a long time, and increasingly so in recent years. The processes of science—investigating, discovering, experimenting, observing, defining, comparing, relating, inferring, classifying, communicating, to name a few—these are what the growth of the mind is all about. The products of science, the knowns and the unknowns, are some of the elements of cognition. Language expands along with understanding. Learning new words, describing tasks, labeling, noting, and recording, all become necessary. Remembering and classifying are most often verbal. Science activities will probably be increasingly verbal with age; communication of problems and solutions is an aspect of most activities. However, physically involved *doing* remains the core of science activities even in the most sophisticated laboratory.

In addition to the self-appreciation already mentioned, further emotional strengthening and social development can result from science experiences. Specific fears can sometimes be relieved with careful and controlled examination of feared objects and how they work. Children sometimes fear animals such as dogs, snakes, or insects. Sometimes they are frightened by machines which are unfamiliar, a record player for instance. Awesome natural phenomena like thunder and lightning, earthquakes, tornadoes, and hurricanes are feared by nearly everyone, but children also can be frightened by rain, fog, and night. The help, support, and attention of an adult who is not unduly afraid can include giving information and planning gradual exposure and investigation, or giving help in sensible coping with the environment. Teachers should give realistic support to feelings of caution about dangerous aspects of any object. Science can relieve fears, but it also teaches cautions. Cautions are based on knowledge and experience. They serve health and survival better than hysteria and disorganization based on ignorance and lack of experience.

Nathan Isaacs has described a less intense, perhaps, but nonetheless disturbing, upset. "Puzzlement is a state of disorientation and at-a-lossness" (1974, p. 95). He points out that young children have early "proto-scientific" ways of organizing what they know about the world. Events then happen which do not fit into their systems.

> But periodically something goes wrong; their proto-science is, after all, still very imperfect and in particular very untested. They are too apt, suddenly to find themselves helpless or hurt because some assumption or belief, implicit or explicit, has collapsed on them. (1974, p. 94)

Seeking answers and finding solutions can give the testing and perfecting that adds confidence as well as knowledge.

Science activities offer great opportunities for group projects. Many experiments are at least two-person jobs. Children often find they need each other's help. Sharing a discovery makes it even more exciting. Science topics give unique ways to aid social growth, too. Concepts of balance, harmony, cooperation, and interdependence can be found in any nature study. They should be emphasized. These are ways in which *all* forms of life coexist and support each other, naturally. It is an emphasis long overdue.

Science is a way of life. Its products affect our lives at every turn. Our society and the world function very differently now from a few years ago because of technological changes. We appear to have incorporated the products of science more enthusiastically than the processes. Problem-solving techniques are basically scientific. Coping with technology requires a great deal of problem solving. I advocate science education on the assumption that people who understand technology live with it better—and maybe longer.

Exploring is fun. Discovering is fun. A problem solved is fun. Laughing, squealing, joyously shared science is a goal worth seeking for yourself and for children. People learn best what they enjoy. Joy also comes through the aesthetic aspects of nature. There is quiet beauty about grass in the wind, a balanced scale, or a bird's feather. There is explosive beauty in seeing heavy bubbling clouds, frost-covered trees, or a group of deer leaping a fence. There is serious, stirring, breathtaking joy in watching red blend with yellow to make orange, whether it is in a sunset sky or on a child's finger painting. The growth of the human spirit is important.

These early beauty-science experiences also form a basis for mature interests in science and in the arts. Certainly they can contribute to a responsible, satisfying growing-up and a life-style that serves oneself and the world well. As Plato said, "All philosophy begins in wonder."

OUR GOALS

The clearer, more sensible, and happier science learnings are, the more likely children are to understand, cope with, and enjoy their lives in the world immediately and in the future. I see it as a package: understand-cope-enjoy, for today and tomorrow—not in linear order, but as a circle.

When we talk about teaching and learning science, these goals for ourselves and children ought to influence everything we say.

2

GETTING IN TOUCH
WITH SCIENCE:
WHAT
CHILDREN DO

Before we think about teaching methods, let's consider learning methods—the activities which bring children and science together. Those are the doings we want to encourage, support, enrich, and, if necessary, plan to teach directly.

Teachers work hard to set up a magnetism display, to plan nature walks, to learn and demonstrate household chemistry. Their immediate wish for children is a simple request: Look at it. (Listen to it. Taste it. Touch it. Feel it. Smell it.) We say, "*Look* at it," or "Look *at* it," or "Look at *it*." Then it turns out to be not such a simple request. What do we ask of a child with three short words? Figure 1 presents some of the processes which might go on in a child as she or he interacts with you, other children, and the objects and phenomena of the environment. Getting in touch with science involves a number of attributes and activities in children. Some have already been discussed. Let us examine some of those highlighted in Figure 1 in a little greater detail, since these are the processes which we want to bring about when we teach science.

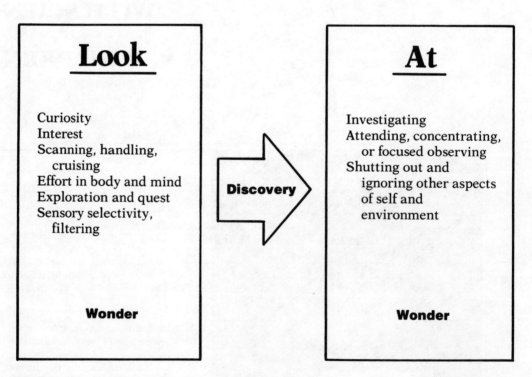

Figure 1. We make a simple request of children: Look At It.

Children Scan, Finger, and Cruise

How do children encounter interesting, but heretofore unknown, events in the first place? If curiosity is an active and deeply impelling force, then how does it work? What happens even before the object or subject or happening has been found or the attention directed?

Children explore first by casting themselves into the environment, by sensory scanning, by fingering and handling, and by roaming or cruising around. Behavior in some children which might be called "restlessness" or "boredom" or "aimless activity" may actually be a kind of looking about. A cruising child will find something. That may be how you tell the difference between aim and aimless, although after the fact. Children explore by running their hands over surfaces as they pass. It is Jeffery, who handles everything in reach constantly, but whose attention is not caught by the things he feels, who needs guidance. He needs to be taught, helped to explore, assured there are findings worth the

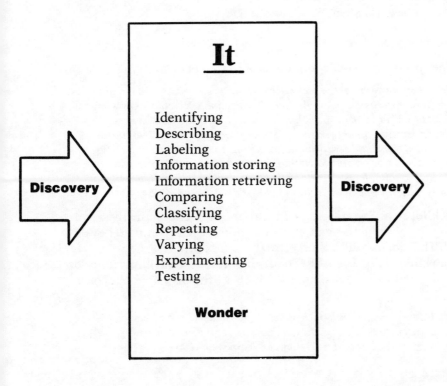

It

Identifying
Describing
Labeling
Information storing
Information retrieving
Comparing
Classifying
Repeating
Varying
Experimenting
Testing

Wonder

Discovery

Discovery

effort. More generally, children who finger for exploration may not appear to be attending, but will be stopped as if surprised by a dip in the surface or a change in the texture.

Children have many and varied ways of tapping into unknowns in their world. This may even be some explanation for why some children seek dark places, enjoy ghost stories and science fiction, and are fascinated by space travel, dinosaurs, and other little-known phenomena. Science is exploration. It begins and ends where it began, circularly, with unknowns. Science is the ongoing discovery of new things, information we did not know, places we have not been, and relations we have not understood or described. Science is, for some, the necessity of going to look for more unknowns. It is quest.

> JULIE: Mom, Rena and I are going exploring.
>
> MOM: Where?
>
> JULIE: I don't know.
>
> MOM: What do you mean? What is "exploring"?
>
> JULIE: Well, we'll just walk around somewhere and look, I guess.
>
> MOM: Are you looking for anything in particular?
>
> JULIE (exasperated): No Mom. We are exploring!

Children Select and Decide

D. Bruce Gardner presents a concept of the child as an open system.

> I see the child as having a very active, selective filtering system. . . . He not only pulls things in from the outside world, he actively participates in choices of what he will and what he will not pull in. . . . Furthermore, I see the child as very active in an executive or decision-making capacity. Here I'm speaking of decisions at all levels, from the most elemental sensorimotor decisions to the most complex symbolic decisions. All the way up and down the line the child actively participates in determining what, among the variety of alternatives available to him, he will do with the sensory materials he takes in from his world. (1971, pp. 63-64)

In speaking of children as "wondering," I mean they are energetically selecting and deciding. They are zeroing in, narrowing down, sharpening. They decide. They find. They focus, but not necessarily in that order.

Frances Hawkins, in *The Logic of Action*, elaborates on the importance of decisions in young children's learning. She defines "the principle of choice" as:

> that given a rich environment–with open-ended "raw" materials–children can be encouraged and trusted to take a large part in the design of their own learning, and that with this encouragement and trust they can learn well. (1969, p. 4)

Children Discover

We have heard a lot lately about discovery. It means children have found. They settle and attend to something uncovered or made obvious to them by their own interests or activities and by their own selectivity. Discovery is the result of a child making a choice, a commitment of his or her senses, body, and mental concentration to stay right at this scene for a while. The moment may be very brief or very long. But it is there, and it is exhilarating.

A part of discovery is the feeling of elation. "Aha! Here it is!" Discovery is a foot-stomper, an eye-widener. It is for shouting "I found it! I found it!" That is what people explore for when they are *exploring*. It is what people observe for when they are investigating. It is what people test for when they are experimenting. Discovery feels good even to adults, as this scientist explains:

> *"I don't know how other people get thrills in life," says one outstanding physicist, "but to me the biggest thrill is seeing a new effect for the first time. It may happen only once or twice a year, but it's worth all the drudgery that precedes it. It's like shoveling dirt in a gold field and suddenly turning up a nugget. When this happens, it spoils you and you'll never settle for less." (Bello 1962, p. 81)*

Figure 1 shows discovery in three places. Each time I see it as a happening, an event, a transaction of the child's selective sensing and deciding, with the environment. Each time discovery emerges from wonder to form a link with other processes which are, in turn, transactions. Each time discovery is creative and fresh. It feels exciting and can impel a child to look again, to stay and learn, to do more.

Children Investigate

Science is being pursued when 18-month-old Tony pokes his finger into the grid work of the air duct because the hole is there. But science is even more. It is wanting to know badly enough to work hard at finding out. When Janet squirms along on her stomach through the tall grass, ignoring the stubble scratches, pushing and puffing, to find out what just went "pip" down there—that is science.

Science activities seek definitions and explanations. Exploration of the object or event which has been singled out is investigation. Investigating means concentrated looking, listening, and manipulating. It may also mean asking questions. It is exploratory behavior with the limits defined by the selection which has taken place.

Children Attend, Focus, and Observe

Science involves aware, focused observation. Zeroing in is a powerful investigation skill. It means children must concentrate, sharpen their pertinent senses, and ignore what is irrelevant or "noise." Children may not only shut out other happenings and objects in the environment but also may ignore inner signals of their own needs which would conflict or divert attention and time. They attend to and focus on the specific activity or object, intently observing and learning. It may be the teacher's job to keep the rest of the world at bay for a few moments and let observation happen. *The teacher protects the learning moment.*

One of the precious provisions a teacher can make is time. A child needs enough time to examine carefully all over and around the surfaces of a piece of granite. A child needs a long turn, or many turns, to see, smell, and feel the sticky budding hickory leaves. Observing with several senses should be encouraged. Seeing and feeling take more time than either would alone. A teacher who intently observes an observing child can be helping a great deal. Feeling the adult's attention and approval encourages a child to continue the activity. Sometimes a smile, a nod, or a comment from you is needed to insure that a particular child will continue observing. Your attentions may distract others. Your judgement is good; you can tell the difference.

Do not be misled by thinking that young children have short attention spans. For years, teachers and researchers were guided by a notion that there was a development of attention span, where the age-related increases in time of concentration were seen as *the* factor. Of course developmental level matters, but other things do, too. The child's individual tempo, whether more "impulsive" or more "reflective," for instance, is being shown to characterize individual style in attention. How long a child plays in the water or manipulates a balancing rig depends also on the appeal of the activity. Does the child *like* balancing rigs? The "stimulus properties" of the object, *in combination with the individual child who perceives them*, figure into the scheme. It depends on all of the background of experiences the child brings to the moment. It depends on how a person is feeling at the time, maybe happy, maybe cranky, maybe too upset to wait for the balancing to take place. It also depends on what else is happening in the situation. If three fire engines roar by under the window, chances are that even the most reflective four-year-old would no longer be playing in the water. However, two-year-olds Evelyn and Tom, both of whom adore water, might still be sloshing away—or if one of them rushed to the window, which one would it be? The combination of many factors describes attention, how it is attracted, and how long it is held.

Exploratory behaviors in general are likely to be stylistic, personal, different by individuals as well as possibly by culture, sex, situation, and, certainly, developmental level. The growth rates of all of the contributing body mechanisms and skills are individual, too (McCall 1974). Your awareness of these personal characteristics in children can help you maximize their opportunities for paying attention to phenomena and for learning to observe carefully without hurry.

Children Identify and Store Information

There is a lot of knowledge in the world. A child's job is to grow up learning a small portion of it, hopefully that part which is most useful to him or her and the world. Generally, teachers worry about children not absorbing those bits of information which have been picked out for them. Science does include learning facts, that is, learning something that others already know. It is one of

life's big jobs, and young children usually accept it with good grace. Children
may find it easier when the reasons make sense because their own activities tell them so, when their own poking and looking uncover information or create the need for it. Teachers can help by making it lively and keeping activities moving. Otherwise, other people's facts can be the dullest things in the day. We can train children from a very early age to hate learning by imposing our facts on them, even when we mean well, when we know they must learn.

Eventually, science becomes a set of adult concepts phrased in adult words. There is no great rush. Concepts and words can come gradually or as a social accompaniment to the child's own involved activities. His or her own discoveries at every step of the way are real and true. They are not contrived or predetermined fact-learning sessions. They are not "lessons." Information first emerges because the child and the earth get together. If that *one adult* is around to share the moment, she or he can also provide the vocabulary for discussion. Then, the discussion adds a way for a child to handle and re-member an experience, therefore to re-experience. Later it will form the basis for organizing and recording experiences.

Children Sort and Classify Information

People acquire many bits of information. Many separate pieces of knowledge could be hard to manage and could lead to confusion and forgetting. Children manage by putting pieces of information together. They compare experiences for likenesses and differences. They put those together that go together. They organize their thinking, their mind storage, and their remembering. A great deal of work has been done to learn about children's classification behavior. See, for instance, Irving Sigel's article (1972). It appears that children group and classify information at young ages and with increasing adeptness as they develop. Classifying the objects and phenomena of the world as you encounter them is very much a part of science.

Margaret McIntyre has been writing a series of columns in the journal *Science and Children* in which she discusses early childhood science educa-tion. Recently, she reviewed some research on classifying behavior in pre-schoolers (1975b). The findings suggested that adults can be helpful, that giv-ing verbal or nonverbal training can facilitate grouping. "The making of classifications by a child requires that he have a criterion by which to group and remember while he discriminates among objects for the purpose of group-ing" (1975b, p. 30). We know that young children also use their own labels, even their own made-up words. And very often, preschool children do not or cannot verbally label a group at all, but will still group objects in a particular way that makes sense to them and to open-minded adults. Adults can suggest the words, or the widely accepted classifications, and still leave room to en-courage the idiosyncratic, unusual ones or developmental ones.

Children like to collect things. A collection is a grouping, a way of classify-ing, too. A teacher, preparing some kindergarten children for a nature walk, hands each child a plastic bag. What do you think the children would do with the bag if the teacher did not say a word?

Children Experiment

The findings of science, knowing that dirt mixed with water makes mud, form the basis for a search for further knowledge. What if I mix sand with water? Dirt with red paint? If I mix dirt and red paint and plant a bean in it, will I get a red bean? Science is seeking causes and being as sure as you can be that you have the right one. It is more than watching it happen, although that is an early step. The process also includes wondering why it happened and trying it out to see if it will happen again. *Repeating an action is an important scientific step.* Scientists and infants in their cribs know that. Repetition is very important to young children. No adult has ever found out how often is often enough, except through an individual child doing the repeating to his or her own satisfaction. Comparing the results of the first time and the second time is the next operation.

Children Compare

Comparison is a significant procedure in any scientific process. It is a special kind of observation. Comparing means examining two or more experiences and thinking about their properties in relation to each other. It is a way of analyzing. Scientific analysis always involves comparing. Even very young children can define similarities and differences. At first, things are mostly either alike or different. When a child attends to details and grows in abilities that aid observation, she or he also begins to see differences in degree. "We-l-l-l-l," says eight-year-old Bertie thoughtfully about a red apple and a yellow apple, "in some ways they're different—but in some ways they are the same." She can name some of the ways, and begin to tell you that some seem more important than others.

Comparison may need memory, if the first instance is gone or must go to make way for the second. If Barton is painting, and mixes yellow paint and blue paint on his paper, he can still compare the resulting green with the blue and yellow in separate jars near his work space. If, however, he pours the blue into the yellow, he will need to retain the image or information of the original colors in his own mental structure in order to make the comparison. Since the latter seems a more difficult operation, teachers can help visual comparison activities by providing the two samples at the same time when possible.

It has also been pointed out that often comparisons in some senses, literally, are easier than others. Vision and touch can provide for experiencing two or more instances at the same time. Gerta can compare the temperature of a glass of ice water and a glass of warm water by sticking a finger in each one simultaneously. Lonnie, who is listening to birds calling, must remember the first sound while he waits for a second call, then decide how the first compares with the second. Is it the same bird? Another bird answering? A different kind of bird? It is much more complicated.

The same problem of comparison through a sequence of events is likely for tastes and smells, and for buzzes, hefts, tilts, jolts, and other inner body experiences. It would seem especially important, then, that children be able to

repeat them at their own pace. They should be allowed to resample both or all
instances as often and as long as they need to in order to make comparisons possible. Teachers doing a tasting comparison could include plans for repeating tastes, instead of everyone in the group getting just one taste of each substance. Even a mouth-swishing with water in between tastes would help—that is what the professionals do. (Tastes of different kinds are perceived through different areas of the tongue. Part of strong "taste" sensations of some kinds are actually smelled. Learning to make these fine distinctions of taste, touch, and smell is a long, delicate process. Young children are just beginning.)

A breath of fresh air between sniffs from the "smelling jars" may aid comparison of odors. I recently saw a collection of jars containing powdered cinnamon, garlic powder, powdered laundry detergent, chopped hay, dried mint leaves, oregano, and perfumed bath salts. It was an interesting array— but all the jars were crammed into a shoe box which was passed from child to child. The whiff was sort of a gourmet market's laundry room conglomerate. Just as children need to sample phenomena one at a time, and at their own rates, they also need relief from stimulation. Then they can be ready for more. Teachers taking on the basically important task of enriching sensory judgments need to plan for the time, space, and freshness that such comparisons require.

Children Vary the Conditions

Varying the conditions is a sophisticated experimental procedure. Many children will think of doing it anyway. Some will need help, or at least sanction— yes, it is all right to water the bean with red paint. Go ahead. Try it. Feel free. Varying is based on comparison and, often, on having repeated the instance. "Try it again" leads into "Try it another way." If it seems appropriate, suggest it to a child who does not think of it or does not have the nerve to ask. When the variation is deliberate, the child knows something already about the original conditions, or the usual conditions, and plays with them. What would happen if . . .? Suppose I . . .? Let's try. . . . Experimental variations are purposeful and playful, exacting and exciting, knowing and unknowing.

Children Play and Create

Does this list of children's learning methods begin to sound more and more like what we have heard included under discussions of play? A number of people have been discussing exploration and play for years. Some feel these are different behaviors right from the start in the lives of animals, human and otherwise. Some think the distinction is academic but intriguing. I am emphasizing the playful, open, and especially creative aspects of early scientific experiences. Young children's development matches brilliantly with open, playful inquiry and inference. Children grow well in environments which encourage these activities. You do, you learn, you know. Early childhood science experiences may not be playing in the adult world of distinctions, but they can be playful.

David Hawkins has spoken and written of the "messing about" phase in science. In this playful part of science work, he means that children should be given plenty of time and opportunities to get acquainted with phenomena in children's own ways. He suggests this could be a remedial step with older persons. Older children and more sophisticated science build on this basic mode of encountering and investigating. Hawkins calls it a "generic justification of messing about." He states:

> We are profoundly ignorant about the subtleties of learning but one principle ought to be asserted dogmatically: That there must be provided some continuity in the content, direction, and style of learning. Good schools begin with what children have in fact mastered, probe next to see what in fact they are learning, continue with what in fact sustains their involvement. (1965, p. 7)

His work suggests, then, that there should be a provision for "messing about" regardless of age of scientist.

Brian Sutton-Smith, in "The Playful Modes of Knowing" (1971), distinguishes four kinds of "microknowing," usually called play in young children's behavior: exploration, imitation, testing, and construction. All of these are modes through which science, nature, and the truth of the earth can be encountered. He draws a brief parallel with four theories of truth. You might enjoy reading this and thinking through how each of these pairs—the theory of truth and its associated play mode— is observable in the science inquiries of young children you know.

3

GETTING IN TOUCH WITH SCIENCE: WHAT TEACHERS DO

In schools and centers, teachers (and directors) often tell us, "Oh, science is our worst area. We just don't get around to it." At home, parents are more likely to be surprised if asked what science activities they do. They may deny doing any and virgorously point out that science is the school's job. However, when you consider the broad definitions of science, you find out you are doing a lot already. Do the children play outdoors? Do they watch the sun emerge as the clouds move? Do they run for the puddles? Do they balance along a beam, or curb, or painted line? Do they wait around the kitchen to watch tortillas brown or ask for a chunk of raw potato before it goes in the stew? You, the teacher, show them an uncooked and a cooked piece of potato side by side, or give them a raw piece of potato while you are cooking and then remind them at mealtime what it was like before it was cooked. You are encouraging them to think about the changes made. You are stimulating scientific inquiry, although you are not likely to call it science.

TEACHERS FOCUS ON SCIENCE

Make yourself aware of what you are already doing. Give yourself some credit for it. Respect it. When Cindy is holding her head as her bandana is whipping in the wind, you say "Listen to your scarf. It's snapping. Isn't that great?" But now say to yourself:

I have started a science experience. I have focused Cindy on feeling and sound, on the *effect*—maybe she will think about the cause. I have taken something very personal to this child, right now, and we have shared it. Maybe I have helped her to wonder, instead of being bothered or upset. And I have shown I'm ready for Cindy's response, wherever that takes us. It could be nowhere, anywhere, out to the airport to see the wind sock, or inside to get a bag and make one.

Put a notebook and pencil in your pocket and try to note every time you and a child interact in an event which is essentially science. Note the times you stay out of it, feeling the child is learning most by his or her own inquiry—you need to give yourself credit for those times too. This activity could lead to an interests inventory for each person and a revealing record of where *you* are with each person's science interests. Writing it down helps you to plan for each individual. It also helps you appreciate yourself. You do a lot of science education already. Build your program from there.

TEACHERS PROVIDE THE SETTINGS

Teachers plan, prepare materials, arrange rooms, and schedule events. You need to be a genius at timing and procurement. You inventory, order, scrounge, repair, and certainly try out the equipment. If you are working in a school, you probably do all of this during the last week of August, along with training, meeting new staff members, finding out the windows in your classroom will not open, and filing no fewer than seven completed forms at the office. If you are at home or in a day care center, you may not have this seasonal upheaval—you have some of it all the time. How does science fit in? You plan for it. You put it high on your to-do list, and you *do* it.

You Inventory the Equipment and Material

What do you need on hand in order to have a science program? The real answer is "time and interest in doing it." No piece of equipment is essential, but a lot of things help. The more limited your natural setting is, the more you will have to bring into the classroom. (We are still working on canned snow to ship to you in southern Florida!)

Table 1 is a composite list of classroom equipment and materials. I have chosen things that are usually accessible and seem appropriate for young children. Sourcebooks and activities resources are cited in the Bibliography (p.131). If you work with older children, you may wish to extend the list. Many of the resources include more elaborate equipment appropriate for older children.

Table 1. Equipment and Materials to Facilitate Science Experiences

Small, General Equipment

Mirrors—framed or encased portable,
  —full-length wall size,
    preferably movable
Magnifying glass—sturdy frame, good
  lens, protective case
Lighted Magnifier
Flashlight
Magnets—varying strengths, horseshoe
  and bar types
Compass—magnetic type, in case or
  with lid
Pocket knife (teacher only) with screw-
  driver and corkscrew attachments
Scissors—blunt (larger pointed scissors
  for the teacher only)
Tongs, tweezers, forceps
Rock pick (also called geology hammer)
Tools—screwdrivers, hammer, pliers,
  level, saw, tip snips, etc.
Plumber's Grabber—for planting bottle
  terrarium, cleaning drains,
  extracting small samples for study
Safety goggles—child size, several pair
Asbestos hot mats or space for setting
  hot things
Basins and tubs, washpans

Plastic containers with lids, many sizes
Bottles, plastic, assorted, with lids
Pots, pans, trays, muffin tins
Bowls and cups, plastic or metal
Assorted sieves, sifters, and funnels
Spatulas, metal and rubber
Eggbeater, wire whip
Eye droppers
Tongue depressor blades, popsicle
  sticks
Backpack or shoulder strap kit bag
Air pump—bicycle, bellows-type,
  and/or camping pump
Mortar and pestle
Kitchen baster, ear syringe, other
  suction devices

Measurement Equipment

Thermometers—metric (reading
  centigrade or Celsius), or metric-
  Fahrenheit combination; and maybe
  an indoor-outdoor set; a wet bulb-
  dry bulb hygrometer; cooking thermometers: meat, candy, oven types
Meter sticks and rulers
Metric tape measure
Metric bow calipers

Metric volume capacity measures
Metric weight set
Avoirdupois weight set
Scales—balance type; kitchen type; bathroom type or human platform scale if available; hanging type for small items (postage scales)
Cooking measures—spoon sets, cup sets
Clock, preferably with second hand
Timing devices—kitchen or laboratory timer(s) to measure seconds, minutes; and maybe a stopwatch, a sand hourglass, or an egg timer

Very Special Equipment
(Can be borrowed as needed, much is for older children or adult use)

Binoculars
Telescope
Microscope
Periscope
Camera, especially Land-type, or "Polaroid" for children's use (sparingly)
Tape recorder
Record player
Radio
Dissecting kit
Portable greenhouse
Vacuum cleaner, tank type preferred
Ice cream freezer (crank type)
Food grinder

Animal Equipment
Cages, boxes, tubs
Food disher, water bottles, exercisers, etc., for rodents
Aquarium, filter pump, light (may also need thermostat and heater)
Small fish net
Insect cages or jars
Insect net
Terrarium—large jars or tanks, screen for tops of animal terrarium, container for water pool, gravel, charcoal, soil
Assorted glass or plastic jars, lids
Bird houses
Bird feeding station; hummingbird feeder if appropriate
Appropriate food, watering, bedding, nesting, sheltering, and tunneling materials

Garden and Plant Equipment
Flat boxes, tubs, or trays
Plant pots, boxes, egg cartons
Saucers, lids, small flat trays
Hand tools—trowel, fork cultivator
Large tools—spades, hoes, rakes, etc.
Growing bulb lights and fixtures
Watering cans
Outdoor hose
Fencing if necessary, or large truck tires, etc., as enclosures

General Materials
Paper and notebooks
Pencils
Wax pencils
Gummed labels
Plastic and paper bags
Paper rolls and spools
Cardboard tubes, carpet rolls
Newspapers
Tape—masking and cellophane
Assorted corks, plugs, stoppers, lids
Clamps, clips, clothespins, paper clips
Rubber bands, wide assortment
String, yarn, fishline, heavy and light
Kite string
Thread
Rope
Assorted springs
Wire, assorted weights, some insulated
Pipe cleaners, bag twist wires
Nails, tacks, screws, bolts, nuts
Hooks and screw eyes
Washers, assorted, rubber and metal
Steel wool
Sandpaper
Toothpicks
Drinking straws, paper and/or plastic
Plastic tubing
Wax—paraffin, bees, or candle
Household machine oil
Blotting paper
Filter paper; coffee filters
Wax paper, plastic wrap, aluminum foil
Foam rubber sheeting scraps
Sponges
Cotton balls and batting
Nylon net yardage

Cheesecloth

Planks and boards

Assorted paper products—cardboard boxes, cardboard sheets, filler material

Wood or substitute—pegboard scraps, Masonite and Formica or other plasticized surface boards, sawdust, cedar chips, driftwood, aged wood

Cooking staples—sugar, flour or cornstarch, cooking oil, salt, vinegar, soda, gelatin, etc.

Cleaning supplies—ammonia, bleach, detergent, etc. (for adult use only)

Specimens and Rainy Day Subjects

Stethoscope

Kaleidoscopes, scanoscopes

Locks and keys

Suction cup fasteners

Magnetic fasteners

Latches and knobs

Gears and geared devices

Clocks (to be taken apart)

Switches, bulbs, batteries

Pulley and wheels

Lever devices

Ball bearings

"Slinky" toy

Scraps of brass, iron, copper, tin, aluminum, etc.

Color paddles, transparent color paper, gels, etc.

Sunglasses with various colored lenses

Prisms

Balloons, inner tubes, inflatable pillows, etc.

Pinwheels or windmills

Kite making materials

Weather vane

Wind sock arrangement

Fossils

Rocks and pebbles, rough and smoothed many varieties, local samples

Concrete, asphalt, gravel

Soil samples—clay, sand, loam

Shells—fish, sea and fresh water, especially local

Real cork and real sponge samples

Seaweed, etc., if possible

Mosses, lichens—local if possible

Shells—birds' eggs, insects, nuts, etc.

Feathers, assorted

Fur pieces, assorted

Wool samples, especially raw wool of assorted colors, preferably uncarded

Leather pieces—pig, cattle, sheep, deer, elk, moose, etc.; assorted tannings, sueded and smooth, thick and thin, flat and thong, also assortment of garments, accessories

Cotton bolls

Raw flax

Nests

Seed pods

Conifer cones and sample of needles

Seeds, great variety

Gourds, pumpkin, variety of squash

Bones—assorted, fish, chicken, other animal

Horns and antlers

Natural fiber fabrics—woolens, cottons, linen—variety of weaves and textures

Synthetic fabrics—nylon, rayon, polyester and acrylics—variety of weaves, knits, textures, weights, etc.

Dried plants—flowers, grasses, herbs, etc.

Dried fruits and vegetables—apricots, peaches, pears, prunes, apples, raisins, peas, beans, lentils, etc.

Whole grains—wheat, oats, rye, rice, corn, etc.

Edible seeds—sunflower, sesame, poppy, caraway, flax, etc.

Edible nuts, in the shells—walnuts, pecans, peanuts, filberts, etc.

Start with an inventory. It actually serves the purpose of reminding you of what you already have and inspires you to think of ways to be sure children get a chance to use it. Special equipment, such as a microscope, camera, or stopwatch can be borrowed for a day or two.

A good glass-lens, sturdy-framed magnifying glass can give new and stimulating perspectives on the world we share.

If you are lucky and have an equipment budget, a good glass-lens, sturdy-framed magnifying glass is a first choice. You should have several if possible. Acrylic hand magnifiers are less expensive, but scratch more easily. Any magnifier should be encased for storage. Most of them do not come that way. Make a case of felt, leather, or other scraps; the children can help. A lighted, pocket magnifier (found at a notions counter) has special uses.

Magnifying lenses do much more than make things bigger, although they obviously do that, too. Magnifiers seem to have a special focusing and observing value. Children can easily compare the object of their attention naturally and magnified. Later they will understand microscopes and phenomena they can see *only* under magnification. Because they can frame and enhance a small area, magnifiers give extra information and aid the investigation of a limited space. Discovery of new phenomena becomes possible. We often hear that magnification opens new worlds. I prefer to emphasize that it gives new and stimulating perspectives on the one world we share. We hope our understanding of the world is enriched by our ability to see a portion of it enlarged. New beauty is revealed and experienced. Because a child's own scope is enlarged, his or her self-image may be magnified also, as a person who sees greatly. Many children seem to identify or affiliate with small objects. The child with a magnifying glass becomes a person who perceives and knows something special, hidden from ordinary view, and personally wondrous. In the following example, several of these processes seem to be taking place.

> When the children arrived at the center in the morning, a hand magnifying glass had been laid out. As the four-year-olds examined it, Mr. O'Donnell made himself available for discussion.
>
> JEAN (*of her hand*): "Oh! I can see right through the glass!"
>
> BOBBY (*of his decorated belt*): "I can see the pictures. It looks different."
>
> MR. O'DONNELL: "How does it look different?"
>
> BOBBY: "Well, it's bigger."
>
> RICKY (*of a picture in a book he was holding*): "Yes, it's bigger, too."
>
> Patty came up, took a turn looking through the lens at the picture, then at her hand. Making no comment she left the group. Several other children came for a brief turn, and Mr. O'Donnell arbitrated a squabble which arose. Jean and Bobby stayed near, took as many turns as possible. Finally, they were left with the glass. They took it around the room, finding other objects to examine. They inspected tabletops, clothing, some clay, and utensils. They looked at a block with rough edges and found "where slivers come from." They went to the plant shelf under the window.
>
> Mr. O'Donnell encouraged their discussion and repeated examination of a leaf of the variegated coleus. They looked without and then with magnification.
>
> BOBBY: "Hey! It's got little fuzzes."
>
> JEAN: "Let me see. Yes, There. Look, Teacher, it's pretty."
>
> Mr. O'Donnell was pleased to have a turn, and agreed with the aesthetic judgment. Then the children looked at snake plants of two varieties and a philodendron, all of which they classified as "no fuzzes." Jean squealed with delight as she focused on a leaf from the purple zebrina. "Bobby!" she shouted, "this one's got *big long hairs*."

Later outdoors the children examined spring lilac blossoms and dandelions and their leaves. One child found a tiny yellow grass flower. Perhaps most exciting was the discovery of flowers in the moss near the base of the pine tree. No one had seen them before, since this was almost impossible without magnification. The children examined seeds from a pine cone. Then Mr. O'Donnell directed their attention to dandelion seeds. The children blew, captured, and magnified the parachuting seeds. Laughed Bobby, "This one has fuzzes for sure."

Most of the equipment listed in Table 1 has obvious uses. These materials are noted in examples throughout this book, and in some of the sources that are cited. Does thinking about the items in Table 1 give you some ideas for things to do? Maybe some are not so obvious? When you are walking in the park and someone finds a tree with a large hollow, your flashlight and a good look will be safer for you than sticking your hand in, and safer for a resident creature than thoughtless probing with a stick. Flashlights are also a fine material for a take apart—examine—put together—work sequence.

A tube of nylon netting stretched over and hung from a circular wire frame makes a hatching cage for a moth, butterfly, or other insect. Netting also makes a good sieve for sprouting seeds, effective scouring material, and an interesting texture experience. Try making your own aquarium or insect nets. Net is handy for covering jars in which living specimens are temporarily detained for observation.

Grinding with a mortar and pestle is a slow way to make flour or peanut butter, but children can participate and observe clearly a basic food process. They can learn the process as it is used around the world. If you have access to grinding stones, it is even better. Herbs and spices release their odors and flavors strongly when freshly ground, and sunflower seeds release their oil.

You Use the Metric System

If each child had to invent a measurement system, what do you think it would be? Would each child's be different? Or would large numbers of children come up with the same idea? Measurement is based on counting. What do young children count? I think a system based on fingers and toes would be commonly invented by children. These sets of digits are, after all, easily visible, give immediate physical and visual sensory feedback, and are repeated on the child's body in obvious and manageable sets of ten. We use the term *digit*, which originally meant finger or toe in the English language. The word also came to mean a number under ten because of the extensive use of fingers in counting and calculating. If a child worked out such a humanly sensible scheme, one based on sets of ten, she or he would have reinvented the metric system of measurement.

The metric is a decimal system. Learning the beginnings of arithmetic computation on the abacus fits well, since this too is based on using tens. The United States is the largest of the five countries in the world clinging to the imperial or English system (the others are Ceylon, Liberia, Malawe, and Sierra Leone at this writing). *Metric is the universal measurement system of all science*, even in the United States. American elementary school curricula are begin-

ning to incorporate metric measuring and seek to establish metric understanding in children. Young children today should grow up using metric as
their basic measurement system. Theirs will be a metric world. This means
today's teachers and parents are the ones who have to change and learn some
new ways. Metrification is *our* job.

Helpful materials are appearing on the market, and there should be more
with time. A publication which gives adults a no-nonsense metrification aid is
entitled *Think Metric Now! A Step-by-Step Guide to Understanding and Applying
the Metric System* (Hartsuch 1974).* A scientific supply company would be a
good place to obtain metric equipment, such as those items listed in Table 1.
Recent catalogues of some of the early childhood education equipment com-
panies from which you might be ordering puzzles and pegboards are also
featuring metric materials.**

For older children, books are now being produced which explain the metric system, for example, *The True Book of Metric Measurement* by June Behrens
(1975). Look at the children's section of your public library.

Young children observe adults measuring, counting, and accounting—
hopefully in metric. The foundations are laid for understanding measurement
and the need for it. Margaret McIntyre (1975a) suggests some informal
measuring activities for young children using everyday materials. It is easy for
children to see how important these activities are in our society. As part of
children's growing interest and abilities in systematic description, arrangement, and problem solving, measurement will begin to come in handy. When
that need arises, you can be there with a system which makes sense to children,
the metric system.

You Gather, Scrounge, and Make Equipment and Materials

If you are starting from scratch, you can see that many of the items listed, and
discussed throughout the book, are wastebasket retrievals or on loan from the
kitchen drawer or arts-and-crafts cupboard. Many of the sources cited tell you
how to make what you need. Colton and Richtmyer's book (1975), in addition
to discussion of inventory and activities, gives photo illustrations and good
do-it-yourself suggestions. We quote two examples:

> *WATER PRISM: A mirror leaning against the inside of a water-filled container (a
> plastic shoe box will do) makes a good prism since light rays can be made to pass
> through a wedge of water when they are projected onto it. (p. 18)*

> *A SIMPLE BALANCE: A very delicate little balance is made from a drinking straw
> pierced through its point of balance by a pin, with small squares of thin cardboard
> slipped in at either end as balance "pans." Discs cut from paper or cardboard with
> a paper punch make satisfactory weights. (p. 30)*

---

* For teachers, see *Metric Is Coming*, published by the National Science Teachers Association
(1201 16th St., N.W., Washington, DC 20036), Stock no. 471-14662, $.75 plus $.50 for handling.
** Send for a catalogue from: Edmund Scientific Co., 402 Edscorp Bldg., Barrington, NJ 08007;
this company has a line of conversion aids, too. Catalogues are also available from: The Judy
Co., 250 James St., Morristown, NJ 07960; and Childcraft, Education Corp., 20 Kilmer Rd.,
Edison, NJ 08817.

A particularly helpful reference is the UNESCO sourcebook (1962). It was designed to be used anywhere in the world by people who do not have much access to fancy equipment or budgets to buy it. The UNESCO sourcebook emphasizes the value to children of helping to scrounge, devise, design, and build what is needed:

> *Believing that science and the scientific method of problem-solving should play a significant role in any modern educational scheme, Unesco [sic] offers this book in the hope that it will assist science teachers everywhere in their important work. The point of view taken is that science is most effectively taught and learned when both teacher and pupils practise the skills of problem-solving by engaging in group and individual study. The devising of experiments and the improvising of simple equipment for carrying them out should form no small part of such study. Thus, the present book includes instructions for the making of many pieces of simple apparatus from materials usually found in almost any region. It also proposes a wide array of science experiments from which a teacher may select those most suitable for providing the observations upon which effective learning may be based.*

> *These improvisations should not in any manner be regarded as makeshift. The experiments and the exercise of constructing the apparatus are in the best traditions of science teaching. Many of the great masters of science have used such improvised apparatus and many of the great discoveries have been made with improvised equipment. (p. 9-10)*

Devising and making-do are some of the more creative human endeavors. You are one of the early childhood persons who do it so well. Give yourself credit for it.

You Furnish and Arrange the Room

I am discussing equipment first so that you can think of why certain arrangements are suggested and how much storage might be needed. I know it happens the other way around—you work with what you have. Whatever space you have is not enough. Your facilities are far from ideal. Early childhood teachers are not only among the world's best scroungers, they are also ranked among the great devisers. It is a precious and proud tradition.

You may want to designate and preserve a "science area," if only to help you remember to keep it fresh and interesting. It becomes a part of your territory which has purpose and identity.

It is usually suggested that the indoor science area be located in a quiet spot out of the main flow of traffic. If you have such an area, you probably want to use it for many purposes. You will have to choose your own priorities. Most of us do not have the luxury of single-purpose space. Fortunately, science works in with many other activities. As you locate, you may want science equipment near the book rack or bulletin board so space can double for a quiet reading area or general resource center. You may need to locate near storage shelves, a cupboard, electric outlets, a window, or other fixtures. Consider the floor covering of the area; it should be washable.

Near a kitchen at home or in a center is good space for science, because the kitchen has some important facilities. A sink, or some water source, is often needed. Whether this is also a water play table, a washtub, a hose and drain, or a bathroom lavatory, area-sharing is possible. Both heating and cooling operations will become a part of a good science program as it grows. Ideally, you would have access to a range with top burners and an oven, and a refrigerator with a freezing compartment. Don't overlook the possibilities of a hotplate, a radiator or hot air vent, the sunshine through the window, an ice bucket, a picnic cooler, or a snowbank as heating and cooling devices.

Lighting should be a major consideration. Good lighting may attract children to the area, as well as enhancing their visual perception when they get there. A table or shelf under a window offers not only good daylight, but the best place in the room for plants and indoor gardening. The animals you keep like some daylight and a little sunshine, but not without some shade. You should also be ready to fix special or spot lighting as needed, for example for a microscope. For this and other equipment, you will want accessible, and high, electric outlets, appropriately capped with safety, turn-and-plug sockets. A lamp with movable spotlighting, a gooseneck or extensor style lamp, could be clamped to a table or shelf for a flexible source of light. You may find use for a drop light or trouble light. Be sure the bulb is caged. You may also want to grow plants under a special growing light. They come in either incandescent or fluorescent styles. You may even want to build a tabletop greenhouse by stretching plastic sheeting over a box or a tentlike frame. A growing light across the top beam of the frame helps but you can also put your greenhouse near a window. It retains moisture well, in dry or winter air. If you have the space, I recommend it. It makes indoor gardening exciting and special, also successful.

Of course tables and open shelves are helpful. Flat surfaces are needed for display and observation, storage, and working. As you set up an aquarium, terrarium, or animal area, you will need protected space and strong supporting shelving.

Projects in a good science program will grow in size and kind. A flexible use of the indoor area can help you to accommodate new interests and ideas. Children will group together to do projects. Popularity of the science area is, after all, what you hope for. The *space* you leave in your science area may be the most important furnishing of all. There should be enough for everyone.

It appears to me that the traditional "science table" in some schools might well be subtitled "The Study of Dust." What can we do to get the area back in circulation? Maybe the quiet area out of the flow of traffic is NOT the best place right now. If you have spent a good part of the year with children bypassing the science table on their way to the block corner, you are ready to set up something different for science. Perhaps getting your display off the science table is worth a try. How about a science cave? A science booth? A science theater? A science dispensary, tent, or store? A science trailer, wagon, or pushcart? If you provide proper lighting, the possibilities are great. Large appliance and sofa crates from a furniture store with a light or lamp inside make a novel science area. If you have a battery-powered camp lantern, you can hang it anywhere. Think about a puppet theater for child-conducted (or puppet-conducted) science demonstrations. Think about taking a large upright crate with a small table inside and cutting a viewing window and two holes for a child's arms, all at appropriate child height. If you can light the inside, a child can put her or his arms through, and use the balance scale or the magnet set on the table working like the nuclear scientists pictured on television.

See if you can get a local laboratory or industry to donate a few old lab coats, the white coats full of acid holes and chemical stains. That is why used ones are more valuable. Scientists of both sexes really do wear them. Young scientists of both sexes will enjoy it, too. You should be aware that white lab coats may carry the association with painful medical experience for a few children. Introduce their usage sensitively.

Because you know about varying levels of maturity, you will plan to reserve some equipment for use under adult supervision only. You need an adult science cupboard where hazardous, complex, or borrowed equipment can be kept out of young hands when not featured and tended by an adult. This is the place for microscope, dissecting tools, camera, knives, and the rock pick.

You Plan Outdoor Learning

Defining outdoor science activities may be a neglected art. What you can do depends a lot on your local circumstances. Take advantage of whatever is available outdoors. Virtually all of it can be "science." Even if you share grounds with other groups, you may be able to claim a little gardening space and a domain for other long-term science projects, such as weather experiments. Ideally, you would be able to flow in and out of your physical facilities with only rare weather restrictions.

Think also about switching. Activities usually done indoors gain new meaning and joy given an outdoor perspective. Is a magnet attracted to the fence? To a brick wall? The outdoor setting also provides better lighting as a rule than any you can provide artificially. Bring the wood shavings outside and have another look. Reversing the usual outdoor setting is also novel. A finger food picnic on a blanket spread in the semidark coatroom can add new dimensions in texture and taste discriminations during an indoor day. Start with the presumption that any science activity can be done either indoors or outdoors. You will not find too many exceptions. But you do the activities differently and you plan differently for them.

If you provide for similar science experiences *both* indoors and outdoors, you may be providing for individual learning styles. Setting may matter. Laurie may be just too busy running and chasing outdoors to see the ladybug spread its wings, even if you call it to her attention. Try bringing the ladybug indoors and sharing it at storytime. Chances are that Laurie will be in the front row. (Remember to share with children the responsibilities of letting the bug go outdoors.) If you provide for repeating activities indoors, and then outdoors, you are providing the repetition learning and learners usually need. You also add variety to your program very simply.

One way of building concepts is by placing the same events or objects in different settings. One way of experimenting is to vary the setting and observe the effects. One way to support the acquisition of Piagetian conservations is to help a child experience substances, weights, numbers, etc., in a variety of settings. Suppose children in the primary room are interested in measuring each other's height with the meter stick. They may even want to chart this information or lie down, draw around each other with chalk or crayon on large paper, and measure the silhouette. Later, they can take the meter stick outdoors; the charts and silhouettes could go too. Aha! José finds he is still the same height—unless he's wearing a hat. Then what? The children or the teacher may initiate a new avenue of search if someone starts measuring shadows. That is an added outdoors feature, and measurements will vary, of course, with the time of day and year. Eventually, José will find out his own body height varies mostly in one direction, with growth he gets taller—indoors or outdoors.

Hopefully, you will have a digging area. Periodic watering may encourage earthworms and vegetation in some parts of the country. A water spigot and a very long hose is a good yard facility. You may want to section off and fence an area where small animals—sheep, goats, pigs, for example—can be kept and allowed to roam. You may be able to have a small animal shed or some animal cages which are permanent outdoor structures. You could have a rabbit hutch, pigeon or chicken coops, or ducks and a small pond. You may at least want a small portable enclosure (e.g., an old playpen with screening around it) to keep the guinea pigs from wandering under the climbing frames. Don't forget birdhouses—be optimistic.

It is convenient, and facilitates a good science program, if you have equipment handy. An outdoor shed can store garden tools, tubs, cages, pots and jars, insect nets, and provide sheltered outdoor conditions for experiments. A shed is also a good place to mount a weather vane and a wind sock. A flat roof, or shelf, on the outside provides a level area where snow and rain measuring devices could be set up. Eventually, you and the children might build a weather station, a windmill power plant, or a solar energy system. Your outdoor thermometer should be large, easily read, mounted at children's eye level in a conspicuous place, and metric. A metric thermometer reads a centigrade, or Celsius, scale. It is nice if you can mount one to be read from inside, too. Or use an indoor-outdoor set-up on a window frame. If one of your several thermometers reads from a Fahrenheit scale, teachers will be comfortable and children will learn history.

Gardening offers many possibilities to children. You are lucky if you can designate and protect an area to make a garden, using organic enrichment of the soil and many experiments. More ecological aspects will be discussed later. In your playground is a good place to begin to live personal ecology as the basic science for young children. An article by Phyllis E. Lueck (1973) describes her planning of a newly remodeled nursery school yard in Guelph, Ontario, Canada. The entire publication offers great ideas for developing a center's playground. I would like to share with you the ways gardening was used as an enhancement to many aspects of this particular outdoor learning environment.

One of the most prised possessions we have in our play yard is a native garden. It is off in a corner which gets good sunlight in the spring and much shade in the hot summer. The reader may be assured that no one has gone on forays into the woods to get our treasures; rather they have come from areas that are being cleared for new development projects. Our aim is to rescue native flowers which would not survive otherwise. The children are delighted with the names as well as the flowers, e.g., lady slippers, johnny-jump-ups, jack in the pulpits, windflowers, foam flowers, and trilliums (the provincial flower of Ontario). Children are intrigued by the uncurling of the fronds of the ferns. One of our young native bushes that promises to have an interesting seed pod in another year is the rattle rush. As the name implies the seeds rattle within the pod when it dries. This L-shaped area is enclosed by a wire fence so that it is "look and see" only for the children at this point.

The other garden areas are in the process of being developed. We expect to have a variety of bushes, shrubs, and vines which will provide excitement for preschoolers. In order for the children to have an opportunity to pick and taste, we plan to have raspberry, gooseberry, and strawberry plants. Coinciding with these will be some bushes with bitter tasting berries so that the children may learn not to taste any berries until they first ask an adult. Our hope is that the honeysuckle may attract hummingbirds. We were unsucccessful in getting any birds in our bird houses this year.

Space has been allotted for a garden where the children may plant some vegetables and flowers. Suggestions that we expect to try are scarlet runner beans with their beautiful flowers, green beans, a couple of stalks of pop corn, a hill or two of potatoes, a tomato plant, perhaps a cabbage or two, as well as the usual carrots, turnips, and radishes. If we are lucky we may get a potato bug or a cabbage worm. We have another spot set aside for an herb garden with lemon thyme, peppermint and the like. Flowers that are meant for picking are planted, e.g., pansies, petunias, snapdragons, and bachelor buttons. In the future our budget will include the cost of a few bulbs for early spring blossoms such as snowdrops, crocuses, and grape hyacinths.

Some of our trees have been mentioned already, the weeping mulberry and the sugar maples. The sugar maples were tapped this spring for the first time. The boiling of the first batch of sap ended in disaster, but the second batch produced a pitcher of lovely syrup which the children ate on silver dollar pancakes. Black and gray squirrels visit us to gather nuts from our hickory tree. The only tree that has been added is a pussy willow. My experience has been that young children are introduced to pussy willows in the spring but usually are not aware of their origin. If there is ever space for another tree, my choice would be one which produces an interesting seed pod such as the Kentucky coffee tree, the black locust, or the yellow wood. (Lueck 1973, pp. 126-127)

What a rich environmental learning experience for these southern Ontario children! But suppose your school is in Arizona? You might be watering a lemon tree or making shampoo from a yucca plant. If you tried, you could find an experience for each of the above and make a transposition for your own

Gardening can enhance many aspects of the outdoor learning environment.

area, seasons, and native plants and animals. What is important is *children experiencing their own habitat fully.*

If you recognize the science aspects of equipment, you can be ready to help children learn elementary physics on the playground. Because the yard is used for large muscle activities, do not think it stops there. Children learn science through their biceps, too. There is solid evidence suggesting that children learn a great deal more through gross motor activities than many of us have realized. It seems likely, and in line with my assumptions, that the physics concepts of energy, motion, friction, work, ease, pace and rate, space and direction, gravity and balance all center and begin within the child's body. These concepts are based on personal kinesthetic experiences. A whole background of perceptual-motor living comes to the situation when Maria starts the toy truck at the top of the inclined plank and runs to the bottom to catch it. She feels inside what is happening. She has been down a slide. She can anticipate, or infer, what will happen to the truck. She knows.

Playground and park equipment, no matter how unimaginative, can serve science learning well. Playground physics means knowing the teeter-totter is a balance scale, the child on a swing is a pendulum bob, the slide or board leaning against the box is an inclined plane ready for velocity studies. Pedaling a tricycle is producing the energy to make the machine run. It will run more efficiently if the wheels are round, if the surface is flat and hard, than it will if the tire is worn in one spot and the surface is mud or sand. Having a variety of surfaces to ride on provides a lot of learning (Lueck 1973). When children notice these phenomena—and they will—that is the time to link their observations with other energy studies or to enhance the understanding of the scientific concept involved. Like this:

Julius was swinging, one of his favorite activities. He pumped skillfully, and wore a layer or two off the soles of his tennis shoes starting and stopping. Today Ms. Jones watched him a while and then sang, "Swing, swing, tic toc."

Julius laughed, "What d'ya think I am, a clock?"

"No," said Ms. Jones, "but you are running like one. You are like a pendulum bob—swing, swing, tic toc. You're the pendulum, not the clock."

Julius's tennis shoes ground him to a stop. "What's that thing?"

"A pendulum? It's something that hangs from a string or a chain or loose-like, and can swing. See? I'll make one with my arm," said Ms. Jones. She straightened her arm, hanging it loosely from her shoulder, and gave it a push with her other hand.

"Oh, I can do that." Julius hopped from the swing. He was not one to resist a physical challenge.

"Great," said Ms. Jones, "can you make one with your leg?"

Julius could. "See? See?" he shouted.

"It's Julius the Great! That's hard to do. You are good at it," said Ms. Jones.

Later, in the kindergarten room, Ms. Jones found some string and a screw, a plastic packing wiggle, a round tinker toy, and a crayon to use for weights. By then, she and Julius had attracted three other children, with Julius teaching each one how to do arm and leg pendulums. One child, having been told about the swing, said she could build a swing stand with tinker toys, so that was done and the children attached the string pendulum. They tried different weights, put them different places, pushed, pulled, and blew on them. Later, the group went up to the principal's office to see the large old Regulator clock with its pendulum swinging away the school day. Ms. Jones was sure she saw Julius swaying in synchrony, whispering, "Swing, swing, tic toc. I'm the pendulum, not the clock."

Another activity that could draw a crowd would be the making of a Plumb Line Hat (Fig. 2). Ms. Jones could be ready to set that up tomorrow, if she would like to see the experiences developed more, and correctly assesses the great interest some children have in the topic. A gravity pendulum, such as a playground swing, is a plumb line in motion. Plumb lines are used to assess up-and-downness, vertical direction. When not moving, the bob, or weight at the end of the string, is straight down, because of gravity. Carpenters and builders use plumb lines to determine whether the studs in their constructions are perpendicular to the earth's surface. Children can, too. Sailors and scientists measure depth of water by using plumb lines. Children can, too. [And if Mom is "plumb fed up with all that noise," it means she is downright, absolutely straight-to-the-center-of-the-earth fed up. It would at least behoove children to understand that.]

The bob is usually made of heavy metal. A fish line sinker is a plumb bob. Children playing fish over a barrier at school are using plumb lines, or if they are not, their lines are waving in the wind. Ms. Jones and the children could take their inquiry in that direction.

Figure 2. *A Plumb Line Hat.*
String attaches a yarn pompom
to a hat at about chin level.
Brim of hat must be broad enough
to allow child to see the string and
pompom while child does many
different body motions.

The Plumb Line Hat in Figure 2 is a western style hat from the drama corner. It is useful because it can be fixed firmly under the child's chin. Any tie-on, broad-brimmed hat would do. The line attached is a string. The weight must be soft and harmless because it may hit the wearer or someone else. A yarn pompom is indicated. A wad of cotton batting or a styrofoam or ping pong ball would work. The wearer can see what happens when his or her body is in motion. What happens when his or her head is tilted? When he or she leans to the side? Gets on hands and knees? Lies down sideways? The position of the plumb line is an indication of whether or not the wearer is standing up straight. What happens when the wearer walks the balance beam or veers around the corner when being pulled in the wagon? This is only one way children enlarge their concept of gravity and themselves in relation to it. Everything they do can supplement the learning because most things that happen to them have a gravity aspect.

The experience of Julius and Ms. Jones might have led to the development of a concept of different kinds of clocks or timekeeping. They might easily have pursued the sources of friction, beginning with the soft squeak of the swing up at the top, linking it to the friction of the tennis shoes pushing to start, resisting to stop. In this case, they might have gone on to look around for other friction points on the playyard and the noises made when they worked. They might have found the gate opening and closing, the pedals going around on a tricycle, the scraping of the boards on the boxes.

If Julius is also a woodworker, this would have been a good time to notice what sawing and sandpapering do, and to talk of friction and wearing away. It could take their attention to the teacher's coat with the fleece worn off around the pockets and under the arms, which, in turn, could take them back to Julius's sneakers or the knees of his jeans. It could take them to the smoothed dips worn into the steps up to the school door. It would be a good thing to relate to an explanation on how chunks of rock get to be beach pebbles.

For Julius and Ms. Jones, there will be other days.

You Develop a Portable Science Kit

You may share yard facilities with a three-unit public school or you may not have a playyard at all—hopefully there is a city park nearby. So develop your own portable indoor-outdoor science kit. It will be handy for field trips, too. Try a shoulder bag or backpack, since teachers of young children need both hands free. Plan and pack different equipment depending on your geography, community, the season, and what you anticipate for the outing. A basic kit could contain:

Magnifying glass in a case or wrapped in soft cloth

Thermometer (metric) with string loop for hanging, also wrapped

Tape measure or tapeline (metric)

Transparent plastic bags and twist-close wires (recycle food sacks. Transparency is important; children need to see what they collect, check on its condition, etc.)

Transparent plastic jars or containers

Sharp pocketknife with screwdriver and corkscrew attachment (for teacher only)

Mirror in a case or wrapped

Flashlight

String, tape

Cotton or soft cloths

Small garden trowel or large sturdy spoon

Paper and pencil

You may add a compass, windmill, hanging scale, insect net, prisms, binoculars, field guidebooks, a rock pick, and/or many other things from time to time. You will probably also add tissues for runny noses, filtering, wrapping, and other necessities which serve science and humanity alike. Keep your kit ready. Take it when you go outdoors with children. Having it is the first step toward using it. The children will rely on it to help find the world in new ways.

You Stock the Children's Resources Center

You will make some supplies and equipment available anytime depending on the development and interests of the children. Indoors, open shelving or an accessible drawer allow children to find the magnifying glass or a piece of blotting paper when they need it for their own inquiries. Can you make your informational resources more accessible, too? Many books depend to some extent on pictures, especially field guides. Children too young to read can find an unknown bird in a Peterson's field guide (1961). You will want to find a way to get children in touch with any resource which aids them. Put books and pictures where children can reach them and near a space where they can be used, such as a quiet table and chairs area. Use them with a child when you share a need to know. Suggest looking it up when a child comes to you for answers.

Viola Carmichael, in her valuable book *Science Experiences for Young Children* (1969), presents some appropriate science topics and gives information the teacher should know, suggests class projects, art and craft ideas, and lists resources: teachers' books, children's books, films, and records for each topic. Carmichael's book gives many good examples of activities and resources fitting together to strengthen a child's understanding. The children's resource center can contain books, pictures, and records for children's browsing. Some materials should be put in the science area, materials which supplement and coordinate science experiences, feed the interests of an individual child, or initiate interest for children in a new topic which is current or seasonal. Sometimes a book draws scattered experiences together into a new concept. Many children's books have science and nature themes; it is not difficult to find one on almost any topic. Make use of the public library and the help of its staff.

Films, slides, filmstrips, and videotapes are less likely to be available to teachers or children. At best, these are a special event for most of us. But you can arrange it. Teachers who plan frequent, difficult, and expensive field trips sometimes overlook the relatively easy audiovisual supplements to firsthand experience. Audios—records and tapes—are more generally used and available. Commonly used audio aids do not have scientific themes as a rule. Recordings of animal sounds, bird calls, and machine noises are available, however. A few children's records include science themes—classification skills and discrimination of objects, numbers, and color.

Pictures are riches often overlooked. Teachers clip magazines and save pictures for resources. The pictures can be useful for bulletin boards or flannel board stories which have science themes. Can you find 15 pictures of friction points? Pendulums in operation? Indoor plants? Gardening activities? Edible seeds?

Without a large expenditure for prepared kits, good illustrations are hard to find. The best pictures for science purposes are full-color photographs. Reality is important. Since many young children are still not sophisticated about the two-dimensional presentation of three-dimensional experience—looking at pictures—a teacher would be well advised to use a photograph and a real object together. A strawberry and a picture of a strawberry can be placed side by side. A Polaroid camera can be a great help; a child can take and process the picture of the object at hand and compare.

You might also consider collecting good photographic illustrations from journals, calendars, and other sources and protecting them with transparent coverings. Or back them with cardboard and tape plastic wrap around them. Children could use a file of photographs so protected. Or you could use a photograph album with plastic sheet pockets for photos and other pictures. Set it up with clippings, photos of objects, a picture story, or some recent snapshots of the children doing science. What better way to remember these experiences, record them, and stimulate a new phase of inquiry? With an album, you can change or renew the contents whenever you want to share some different pictures.

TEACHERS GUIDE EXPERIENCES

You plan, set up, and schedule science experiences. You also prepare children for them. You bring children and science together using a number of "teaching techniques." Then, your work has only begun. Following up is important. Fitting science into the total curriculum is worth consideration and work.

You Let Science Experiences Happen

It may be the most difficult teaching you do. I have encouraged you to give yourself credit for knowing when to stay out of a child's experience and when to protect her or his experience from interruption.

Lunch at the Head Start center was usually interesting. On this particular day, four-year-old Jolene picked the large chunk of celery from her lunch plate. A string was loose at one end. She pulled it about one-quarter of the way along the stalk, then, holding the string end, suspended the swinging piece of celery. It slanted deeply, hanging nearly vertically. Delighted, Jolene pulled the celery string further, nearly halfway up the chunk. She gently let the piece swing down again. As she watched intently, the piece of celery wavered, slanted, but swung somewhat more horizontally. Jolene looked at the piece again, then carefully took the lower end between two fingers, brought it to her mouth, and took a bite from the end. Testing the swing again, she saw that it now slanted bitten end up. She smiled broadly, bit a very small chunk from the other end, and tested again. Aha! It balanced to her satisfaction, the observer inferred, since Jolene grinned and quickly ate the entire piece of celery.

Jolene learned something scientific that day. She pursued her interest with diligence, creativity, and apparent success. She obviously was observing and comparing. Her testing was controlled and rigorous. Her pendulum experiment in weight compensation and the effects she observed showed considerable inferential process and flexibility in her behavior as it progressed. She appeared to learn something about balance and about the physiology of celery. What would she have learned if someone had said right away, "Don't play with your food"? What would she have gained had someone come along to clear the dishes or wipe the table? The teacher did *not* interrupt to enrich language development. It was educational just the way it happened. A sensitive teacher sat nearby, making sure.

You Figure Out When, Where, and to Whom Science Experiences Are Likely to Happen

Anytime, you say. Yes, anytime and anyone—all the time. But are there some especially *likely* times, situations, and persons in your own center, school, or home? Do you divide your group's day into scheduled events and "free play"? When does science usually occur? Children seem more likely to discover when they have opportunity to cruise, look, and finger. Do they have enough of this kind of time? Are they free enough from interference to build a balancing tower of blocks and to find that large blocks will not fit into small spaces? Are some materials always available to help them discover that, for instance, soap granules dissolve in water but white sand does not? Do they feel free to try it and find out? Even in the bathroom sink? ("Only," says the plumber, "if they have a drain filter." So get a drain filter.)

Examine your center's routines, your conditions, and the groups of persons who get together. Are some groupings of children more likely to produce, "Teacher, teacher! Come quick and see what we found!" than others? Are some children especially likely to initiate inquiry activities? Is your indoor setting richer in science possibilities and tools than your outdoors? Why don't you make a list of the times and places in which science experiences are most likely to happen. Think about the children who do the most finding. Try to figure out *why* those times, places, and persons. Then you can make those conducive conditions available to more children more of the time. Can you discover some clues in watching a group of children who discover and investigate together well, successfully, happily?

You have already been thinking about equipment, room arrangements, and backpack science. *You* make it happen. You arrange the opportunities. You set it up to be discovered when you put three different kinds of seed pods close to each other on the table. When you select objects to put into the water play tub, you are planning science experiences. Teachers encourage inquiry in many ways.

Arrays and Centers. We spoke earlier of children making choices—they select and decide. In a given setting, a classroom for example, they select from what is available. Teachers decide what will be available to children. You have heard or read about arrays or arranging learning centers. It means you put out enough items and activities for all children to have some choices (Hawkins 1969). You plan and do your work ahead of time so children do not have to wait in line for turns or while you set up. You plan so everyone can be busy at a chosen activity. *You have more than one science possibility at a time.* What you put out and arrange has some cohesiveness—it goes together—thus the term *array*. Everything in the room has a purpose which you have thought out. By the time the child chooses, you have already provided the time, space, sanction, encouragement, tools, and an array of activities and materials which make sense for these children at this time in their lives—and yours.

Displays and Attracting Attention: Using Novelty. Teachers set up displays. This is one of the most common science teaching techniques. You lay it out and see what happens. You want it to attract children, not dust. How do we catch attention in the first place? Sometimes material is lively enough to bring a group of children together under any circumstances, for example, a litter of kittens. Most any novel material, something you have not shown before, will catch some child's eye. You can use novelty other ways. Try a new arrangement, an old thing in a new place. If you are all used to "seeing" the fern plant on the windowsill, put it in the drama area. Maybe someone will really look at it. Try a new time. Use the fishbowl and guppies as a centerpiece on the lunch table.

Centerpieces. The lunch or snack table is, in fact, one of the best time-and-place combinations for a science display. Table centerpieces become focal to a somewhat captive audience. If materials are clean, so as to uphold eating hygiene, the contents of the centerpiece can be examined, experienced, discussed, and shared by a group with joy. Traditionally we think of a bouquet of spring flowers, a bunch of autumn leaves, a pumpkin, or a bowl of gourds or pine cones. Beautiful and interesting, it is science at its aesthetic best. How about a basket of rocks, a bowl of nuts and bolts, screws, nails, and balls of aluminum foil?

Science in Menus.   Taking the decor from the food, as well as the other way around, allows you and children to take science from both. Suppose you are having squash for lunch. Arrange a whole acorn squash along with one cut in half—unless you have been able to help the children prepare the lunch squash in the first place. If you are being served peanut butter sandwiches, how about a bowl of peanuts in the shell to examine, open, eat, compare flavors? You can find lots of science display clues in your menus. Your centerpiece may also lead to further inquiry activity after the meal. Can you clear the dishes and get out the magnets? Is there time to cut up and clean the pumpkin and prepare the pulp for bread? Tomorrow, maybe?

Humor.   Another way to attract attention to a display is to add humor. Many young children find incongruities funny. Upside down things are funny. Suspended, swinging, moving things are funny. Anything mixed up or out of place is funny. And anything funny is attractive.

> The kindergarten science table held objects for children to handle and examine: several small freshwater clam shells, a robin's nest, some filbert nuts, a few chips of cedar wood. Over a period of days, several children had looked and handled the objects. On one day, a child asked the teacher about the nest, and they went to look at the tree from which it had fallen. Mostly, though, the display was ignored. Then, one morning, a child burst into loud laughter over by the science table. Everyone rushed to see what was going on. There, carefully arranged, were the cedar chips in stairsteps leading up to the nest. Inside, the clam shells were nestled together, each one with its own filbert inside. We all laughed, somehow half expecting the "Nut Clam Bird" to step right up at any moment. The Nut Clam Bird became a group joke savored for days. It also led to great renewed interest in the objects thoughtlessly displayed together in the first place. And we had to make sure that children knew the difference between the humor of fantasy and the reality. Where did those objects really come from? What did they do? Where were the animals/plants which produced them? How did they get here? It gave us popular and interesting science experiences for days.

> We never found out who did the novel arrangement. We were pretty sure it was not an adult. Believing The Phantom never strikes twice in the same place, we learned a lesson about making science displays.

Simplicity.   Keep displays simple, if you are hoping to capture and focus the attention of young children. One idea, one classification group, one activity at a time in one place is usually enough. Think about the degree of complexity you are actually presenting to a child. Nests, shells, nuts, and wood chips do not belong together by any concrete-thinking child's system. Because these items were displayed together, it was a sensible, if mistaken, inference that they belonged together. It happened there was a relational classifier with considerable imagination. That was unusual. The display was too much, too broad, and presented too many directions to follow. It did not make sense. We were lucky it made good nonsense. But you cannot always count on The Phantom.

Highlighting.   Highlighting techniques do not have to be saved for the parents' bulletin board. They work on science tables, too. Place dark materials on light background, light materials on dark. Use a backboard or drape of soft fabric behind your display material. Spread a contrasting mat under your display or put your material in a contrasting container. Make it noisy. A bowl of beach pebbles is fun; a brass bowl of beach pebbles pulls everyone from the surrounding area. Outline the display with bold strokes. Draw a circle around it. Put up an enclosure around it. Shine a light on it. Put it inside a picture frame or suspend it from a string. Post a large arrow pointing to it. At the door, start a string that leads to it.

Suspense.   Add a note of suspense or impending surprise. If you really want children to wonder and find something, put it in a closed box. Part of the enduring charm of a texture box or feel-and-guess bag is the suspense. Presenting material in a "theater" provides a closed curtain and a curtain time. Putting an article with a distinctive silhouette behind an opaque, backlighted screen may actually help children define clues, as well as being a good game. Putting something in your pocket and providing clues—the shape, noise, smell, color, purpose—may build suspense and information, in addition to focusing thinking. Fanfare may sound unacademic, but it is by no means unscientific. If your science table lacks verve, try a little "ta-dum!" Children like it; you will too.

Being Ready.   Being ready when the moment arises, when a child expresses interest, or when children need something to do, is the best teaching technique we have. I know a teacher who did not feel dressed for work until she had put a science experience in her pocket. It had to be there to spark things indoors or out, when someone needed intellectual refreshment. Mirrors, magnets, magnifying lenses, locks and keys, compasses, are the kinds of things which will fit into your pocket. Even several of each, for larger groups, will fit. More children, more pockets. Can you make a list of five pocket-sized science experiences? If so, you are "dressed" for the school week. To help you get started, we offer you a few suggestions in Table 2. Before you do these activities, see what children will find to do with a wax crayon and paper, a tea strainer and filter, an eyedropper bottle, rubber bands, paper and a small bottle of water. Reserve the following suggestions for later, and give the children's ideas plenty of time to emerge and develop.

Table 2.   Five Pocket-Sized Science Experiences

Sieving Liquids: A tea strainer with a filter paper fitted inside equips children to isolate solid matter from liquid. Whether it is a sample from the fishbowl or from a mud puddle or a melted snowball, chances of children filtering out some solid material are good. Can you identify the material? In an area where air pollution is visible, this may be a good way to illustrate why one should not eat the snow. You may want to use a magnifying lens to see and define some of the found substances. Children can begin to distinguish contaminants (i.e., rust flakes) from congenial matter (i.e., algae in pond water).

Texture Rubbings: Notepaper and pencils or crayons, preferably wax, are all you need. A child can place paper over a surface and rub with crayon to make a picture of a texture, can compare the feel with the visual image of the texture. It works well on wood grain furniture, fence posts, play equipment, rocks, bricks, concrete, asphalt, plastered walls. The results are a way of keeping texture records and comparing textures to each other as supplement to feeling them. Do they look like they feel?

Twanging: An assortment of thick and thin, long and short, rubber bands is all you really need, although a few small boxes would also fit into your pocket. The idea is for children to find and compare sounds. A thin rubber band stretched around a box sounds different than the thick one next to it. Why? They sound different on a large box than on a small one or on an open box than on a covered one. Try bands between two points such as back posts of a chair and around various shapes of containers and containers made of different materials. Place around a fence post and stick or pencil, encourage twanging and listening as the stick is drawn farther away and the band is stretched then relaxed. Make a pocket-sized "guitar" from a popsicle stick and a matchbox.

Attracting Insects: An eyedropper and a small amount of sugar or honey in water will get you ready to feed the insects. A child can place a few drops near an ant hill, can try to draw the attention of a butterfly, can attract insects to the windowsill of the classroom. Children can also observe over a day or two as drops of sweetened water placed in a sunny spot, indoors or out, evaporate. What happens to the sugar, Tomorrow you could try it with salt water or some other solution. Will the ants eat it? Does it leave a residue?

Miniwashes: You can do this with an assortment of equipment. Try a pad of paper and a small bottle of water. See what substances are found to give off color and solid material, dry or wet. Rub some of the substance or object on paper. Wet the paper or object and try rubbing again. Children will find many samples to try, for example, dirt, sand, nuts, pods and pine cones, flower petals, crumpled leaves, stones, sticks, chalk, paper clips, berries, vegetables, shells, nails, and screws. Can you mark with it? Wet or dry? Do the substances change appearance when wet? Regain original appearance when dried? The solubility of various substances can lead to many days of experiments.

Trips. If you cannot bring the experience to the child, take the child to the experience. That is the reason for trips, from a journey downstairs to see the furnace to the annual trip to the zoo. Science curriculum is well served by trips if your trips with children fulfill the goal of investigation. Are time and opportunity for children to discover and inquire written into the schedule? When you plan a field trip, do you think carefully about what children are likely to learn from the experience? Adults sometimes plan more than children can absorb. Maybe we push too hard because we know the experience is rare or expensive, and we want children to make the most of it. A trip to the city arboretum may offer the possibility of seeing more than a hundred different kinds of trees. However, young children may learn more if we go to see a banana tree bearing fruit, or if we go open minded, singing, "There are many pretty trees all around the world,"* and let the children find them.

*Words and music by Ella Jenkins, recorded on Scholastic record album SC7653; publisher— Sheet Music, Forster Music Publisher, Inc.

STAMPS
PARCEL POST
GENERAL DELIVERY
POSTAGE DUE

Walks. You plan field trips to special places in the community—greenhouses, parks, museums, industries, laboratories, and stores—for special events or displays. You can plan special trips around your house or center, too. Walks are any excursions on foot. Nature walks usually mean the teacher intends to concentrate on finding natural objects and phenomena in their natural settings, the woods, the park, or the alley. "Technology walks" to nearby buildings or around the center offer children the opportunity to experience machinery—typewriters, computers, time clocks, fuse boxes, water meters, etc. An excursion to a construction or renewal site also offers possibilities.

Consider whatever is within walking distance. Sometimes children on walks focus in new ways on everyday neighborhood experiences and learn science as well.

Crawls. I wish to consider another perspective. Have you ever gone with children on a crawl? Adults may be limited by what they see at adult eye level, but because you are a good early childhood teacher, you are in the habit of thinking about life and experiencing at a young child's eye level, too—and that is an important perspective to take along on a trip. Rachel Carson is among those who have realized the keen sense of relating to the earth's surface that a small child brings to experiencing small things:

> *And then there is the world of little things, seen all too seldom. Many children, perhaps because they themselves are small and closer to the ground than we, notice and delight in the small and inconspicuous. With this beginning, it is easy to share with them the beauties we usually miss because we look too hastily, seeing the whole and not its parts. Some of nature's most exquisite handiwork is on a miniature scale, as anyone knows who has applied a magnifying glass to a snowflake. (Carson 1965, p. 59)*

I suggest a crawl to acquaint yourself, and share with children, the earth's surface and the life and substance upon it. Outdoor crawls can show you new life and ways of life. A crawl indoors can provide information about flooring surfaces and their properties. Have you ever explored the "underneaths"? Underneaths, the undersides of objects, can give children information about constructions and finishes, for instance. It may also help them to understand and respect these surfaces as something besides a depository for chewing gum. Our cultural system seems to opt for the facade, the surface that shows, as having value. Curiosity, an analytical approach, and respect for wholeness would be fostered by encouraging children to investigate and know the whole thing through all its parts and faces. Science is seeing wholes and parts in relationship to one another. Crawls offer some new possibilities (McIntyre 1975d).

Excursion Techniques. Regardless of the kind of excursion you are planning, there are a few techniques that can help you and children:

THE CHILDREN AND MRS. X WENT ON A FIELD TRIP TODAY
They Had A Wonderful Time! Why?
THIS IS WHY THEY HAD A WONDERFUL TIME

Mrs. X walked the route day before yesterday. She looked for potential dangers and interesting sights.

The group planned yesterday. Mrs. X sat on the floor with a covered basket in her lap. Soon all the children joined her. Several asked if there was a surprise in the basket so she showed them the contents—a labeled sack for each child. Then they planned their walk. When shall we go? Why? Will you need shoes? Why? What shall we take? Why? And so on until the children were restless.

Mrs. X invited helpers. Two school-age children were delighted to go.

She told the parents. Even though she has written excursion permissions, she always shares with the parents so they can share with the children. Some parents need help in understanding how something so simple can be so special.

The children and Mrs. X packed the basket during indoor free play. It contained the children's sacks, cleansing tissues, carrot sticks, raisins, paper cups, a jar of water, a pair of underpants, an insect book, a bird book, and a flower book. (Mrs. X has quit taking insect jars.)

They reviewed the excursion rules. The major rule is to stay away from the curb and street.

The children went to the bathroom just before leaving.

The group walked slowly and stopped frequently. So that Andy could gather leaves, Maria could try to climb a tree, Gina could identify a lady bug, Lisa could show her pebbles to Mrs. X.

They enjoyed a leisurely snack and talk time beneath a tree.

They returned with special treasures such as bird feathers, seed pods and odd-shaped twigs in their sacks.

The children shared with their parents. Most told about the nesting birds they saw.

Tomorrow Mrs. X will probably read a story about children going on an excursion. What do you think her children will have to talk about? (Pitts 1971a, pp. 13-14)

Four diverse resources are especially recommended to inspire your science excursions and procurements. *Experiences with Living Things* by Katherine Wensberg (1966) is an inspiring account of young children doing natural studies and learning ecology concepts through wonder and beauty, with an early childhood science teacher of great skill. The book details the careful planning and thought which go into making a firsthand and first-rate experience for a child with natural phenomena. It describes a teacher who arranges opportunities for learning on the spot. Follow-up classroom activities are also discussed.

We have already referred to *The Sense of Wonder* by Rachel Carson (1965). Because the feeling it imparts is one of sharing great delight in and respect for nature, this book is a good argument for trips in the fields and woods, streets and alleys. It also encourages you to try science trips as all-weather experiences.

In a leaflet published by the Association for Childhood Education International, Judith Bender (1969) discusses the use of natural materials as science learning tools. She lists many experiences with and concepts to be derived by young children from water, snow, ice, fire, mud, sand, clay, rocks, and the terrain: space, contour, surface, composition, and natural growth aspects of the land itself. It may amaze you how much there is to see in a glance around you, wherever you are.

"Opening Up the Classroom: A Walk Around the School" by Sylvia Hucklesby (1971) gives ideas for things to do with stones, sticks, and plants. Some of them will fit in your pocket. All of them will fit in your head, and that is where you need them.

Your own community and geographical region will suggest special places to go and investigations to plan. The above resources take you from the shores of the Pacific Northwest to the Maine coast by way of Urbana, Illinois. Whether you live in rural Mississippi or on urban Lake Michigan, you can find science experiences worth the trip.

Demonstrations.   Sometimes a teacher demonstrates a technique or an experiment while children watch. It would usually reach children as an experience more effectively if they had direct multisensory contact, that is, if they did it themselves. However, there are occasions where demonstrations make sense. Children may feel hesitant about touching a new pet. A borrowed piece of expensive equipment may require a demonstration of its manipulations and functions. Hazards may be judged too risky for children's independent investigation, as with high cooking heat or sharp knives. A teacher will be aware that she or he functions as a model *if* she or he actually does the activities, takes a turn, sets the pace, or gives a vividly illustrated talk on ground rules. Remembering you are a model helps you check yourself. Are you demonstrating and illustrating behavior you wish to teach? You should show or illustrate what *to do*. Never demonstrate what not to do. With young children particularly, we cannot be sure what part of our behavior teaches or what part they will imitate. A teacher demonstrating fire prevention should not be lighting matches.

Talk.   Discussion is a maligned technique, perhaps because it is often misused. Discussion means persons talking together. It does not mean teacher talking alone or asking all the questions. Discussions can effectively add to experience. What makes discussions good and right in enhancing a child's learning processes? How does the teacher help a child learn to communicate about scientific findings? It is not known for sure how a child learns to communicate at all. Many of us have ideas that have worked with some children in some settings. It is assumed that active sensory-cognitive experiencing comes before words and words come before discussions. Children learn a lot of the content and meaning of the language from the actions and words of the models around them. Children appear to use words appropriately when those "right" settings are indicated by adults and other purveyors of the culture(s) of the child's life. We do know the teacher has to talk with the child in the child's mode of communication or there will not be much communication.

Words.   Yes, you *can* use scientific words and descriptive phrases as part of the interested, friendly accompaniment to the child's direct contact inquiries. Please do. Children get used to words and begin to use them casually and in the right place and time if adults do. The phrase *igneous rock* is not any harder to say than *french fried potato*. It is not really so difficult to talk science, but teachers may have to learn how. Your use of the words is not the same as a big campaign to teach them. I think children switch away rapidly when an adult says: "That's the mycelium. Now, say the word: *mycelium*. Repeat after me. Say it again. Mycelium." Did you just mentally file the word *mycelium* under "who cares" before you even found out what it means? If so, I have made my point.

Words which describe scientific activity are important. That is the part children want and need to communicate. Words such as *float, sink, humidify, evaporate, congeal, solidify, dissolve, balance, inflate* express action. That is what children like to do and talk about.

> "Those who can, do. Those who can't, talk," muttered the disgruntled student. "I don't understand what you mean," replied the professor impishly. "Can you show me?"

Sometimes words are necessary.

Discussions.   Teachers can set up discussions or arrange opportunities for talking. Some sources suggest you initiate science experience: "Begin with a discussion of. . . ." I disagree. Begin with a warning if you are going to change the schedule or upend a routine. Begin with an explanation of cautions or safety rules if necessary. Begin with a planning talk sometimes. But begin, if you can, with doing, with children in action, with direct experience. Talk later. Wait with the discussion until children can share it. A teacher who "discusses" findings at a field trip site beforehand, for example, is the only one in the group who knows anything about it. This sets up a situation where children do not have anything to say. They cannot talk about a sandstone cliff or a zebra if they have never seen one. Save the discussion for the time after everyone has experienced, has had a turn, has looked and felt to her or his own satisfaction. *Then* discussion can add a new dimension.

You can encourage children to talk about their images and impressions of phenomena. Your interest, your questions, and your own sharing of your observations in a spirit of delight and excitement can all set the stage for discussion. You can pace talking with your own casual and quiet approach. These are ways you can convey that each child will be listened to even if it takes all day. Nothing is more important. You have to find your own ways to let children know that. Remember, discussion really means communicating—verbal initiating, listening, and responding. If a class discussion group contains more than three or four children and an adult, you *know* who will do most of the talking, and to whom the children's remarks will be directed. Nearly all the children in the class group sitting in a circle around the teacher may or may not be listening, but they are *not* discussing.

Correctness.   Adults who do most of the talking have to know a lot. Even then, there is trouble with the "one right answer—mine" approach to science. Let's consider a lesson on the classification of plant parts. It seems a significant issue to some early childhood teachers to determine whether certain plant parts are fruit or vegetable. The topic appears frequently in collections of lesson plans. It is a good example of why an open (all suggestions welcome) discussion makes sense—because the adult-imposed classification sometimes does not.

   Biologists have definite concepts of fruit, fruiting, and fruiting bodies. These overlap but are not the same as definitions in common cultural use, nor are they exactly the same as those taught to young children in the name of science. This is also true for vegetable. Children are often taught that the fruit is the part of the plant which contains the seeds; vegetable includes all other edible parts of the plant. On the other hand, plants are vegetables, thus fruit is a part of the vegetable. Culturally (and on occasion legally) fruits are a sweet part of the plant usually eaten for dessert, snack, or used for sweet cooking. Vegetables by the same token are those plant foods eaten during the main courses of the meal. My dictionary gives nine definitions of the noun *fruit*—all correct. So who's right? On the teacher's list of fruits, you will find squash, tomatoes, peas, beans, and cucumbers. No self-respecting five-year-old will accept that. And aren't they both right?

   We serve the growth of logical thinking well if we help children eventually learn all these points of view and their different purposes. We add understanding of the relatedness of all natural phenomena, the shortcomings and efficiencies of language and of human defined groupings. There are social problems involved in taxonomy (the work of making scientific classifications), most of which are, in fact, open issues. A reasonable teaching goal is to help children learn there are some scientific problems left to solve.

Misinformation.   What about misinformation? Your first job is to relax about it. Your second job is to figure out what it really means to the child and what the child really means by it. Your third job, if by now you decide it is still appropriate and important, is to find a way to correct the information, not the child.

> Robert and Gladys were watching the fish in the nursery school aquarium tank.
> "Look, the fish has three mouths," said Gladys.
> "Just that big fish, though," added Robert.

The teacher, Ms. Martinez, came up to the tank. "Where?"

The children pointed to the large swordtail.

"What do you mean about 'mouths'?" asked Ms. Martinez.

"Well, there's that one in front that goes like this," and Gladys opened her mouth up and down. "And there's one here and one here." She held her hands near her ears, clamping her palms on and off her head.

"You explain well. I know just what you mean," said Ms. Martinez. "Let's see how the fish eats." Ms. Martinez got food from the cupboard. The children fed the fish, observing the swordtail and other fish in the tank. After some discussion, the children decided the one in front was the mouth since all the fish ate only there. Ms. Martinez said the other two openings were gills; they were really more like noses since that is how fish get oxygen, which we get from air. The aquarium had a bubbling filter, so the children could see air passing through the water. Later, they decided it must be water that went in and out the gills. Ms. Martinez encouraged them to clasp their hands together, dunk them in a sink full of water, and see if they could hold air when they simulated gill action by pushing their palms together, swishing water in and out.

"We are not fish," she explained. "We can't get the oxygen out of the water. We get our oxygen by breathing in air directly like this." She took a deep breath in and out. She thought she would add that, but did not expect the children to understand it completely now.

Misinformation may be set right by planned individual experiences over a period of time. Young children attend best to one topic or dimension of thinking at a time. They are not ready to account for all the information which might be available to adults. Your observation of mistaken concepts may indicate to you a whole new set of experiences for the child or children. Guide them through, one step at a time. Take a clue from Ms. Martinez. At no time were children told they were wrong. At no time were they immediately corrected— their experience was arranged to be self-correcting.

Questions.   Almost any kind of questions may come from children. But what kinds come from adults? What questions do you usually *ask* children? Using questions to stimulate discussion and thinking is a common teaching technique. But it is tricky. Let's examine a few question types used by adults to start discussion and see why.

Question Type 1.   It has a correct answer and persons old enough to be verbal usually know it. For example, "What will happen to your shirt if you pour a cup of water down the front?" Or, "Why do we wear mittens in the winter?" If you take Type 1 seriously, it should be insulting. A question everybody knows the answer to is a challenge only to one's self-respect and an embarrassment for others, unless we are playing a game we all know is foolish, and laugh together.

Question Type 2.   Type 2 has a number of variations. This kind has a correct answer and some people know it, others do not.

- *Type 2a.*   Teacher knows the answer but the children do not. For example, "What do we call this fat part of the worm?" This time-honored technique should be rethought. Why should a teacher, who knows the answer, ask children, who do not, a question? It is not very sensible when you stop and consider the reverence we want to teach for the questioning attitude.

- *Type 2b.*   Children know the answer but the teacher does not. A teacher might ask, "Where did you find that worm?" It may be a legitimate request for information. On the other hand, it may be a Type 1 question in thin disguise. When teachers ask children, "Who had the red truck last?" it is not intended to provoke extensive discussion; everyone knows that.

- *Type 2c.*   Teacher and some children know the answer; some children do not. For example, "Will the worm bite?" Teachers can use this kind of question successfully to begin discussion, if they let the children answer and teach each other. Once such a conversation is started, the teacher may withdraw, children can teach each other.

- *Type 2d.*   No one in the room knows the answer, but the teacher thinks he or she does. For example, "What makes the red line in the thermometer?" (The teacher and most people think the red line is mercury but it is not. Mercury thermometers are expensive, the line substance is always silvery in appearance, and chances of there being one in the classroom are low. The red stuff is usually alcohol.) Questions like this can give education a bad name, if they pave the path for an incorrect authority.

Question Type 3. It has no correct answer, and people know that. For example, "What makes the baby hamster start breathing in the first place?" The response requires some knowledge and a feeling of respect for unknowns. It is a question we can pass on as a question; it belongs to us all in question form. A teacher may teach a lot when he or she answers, "I don't think anyone knows that yet. Maybe someday someone will learn the answer and then we can all share it."

Question Type 4. It probably has a correct answer, but no one in the room knows. "What kind of bird's egg shells are these?" "What do you call this plant?" "Will snow or ice melt faster?" These are questions teachers work to find answers to. They can and should lead you and children to resources to obtain knowledge you all want or need and to experimentation, comparison, and varying conditions. "I don't know. Let's find out" are among the most beautiful words a teacher can say.

Question Type 5. Each person has her or his own correct answer. These are probably the most generally successful discussion provokers. "How do you feel about it?" "What do you think?" "How would you describe it?" "What do you think is important about it?" "What does it look/feel/smell/taste/sound like to you?" "What do you think would be a good way to find out?" The questions stimulate lively discussions. Be sure conclusions are reached by a group, "You all agree it tastes salty?" instead of confirming a single opinion as conclusive.

To summarize, questions are best and most successfully used to start discussion if the teacher does not already know the answer, if there is no generally correct answer, or if the question asks for the opinions and experiences of each person as her or his own authority. If you want to diagnose, be honest: "I want to see if you can tell how many clothespins are here. How many are there?" Otherwise, if you know something and you want children to know it, too, tell them. They will do you the same respectful favor when they have something to tell you.

Analogies. Teaching with analogies is traditional in some cultures. Most of us do not realize how often we rely on this technique. You can aid understanding by showing how one situation is like another, usually one you can experience more easily or know already. The technique builds on children's observations and understandings of similarities and differences and on the ability to make comparisons. For example, it is hard to explain to young children how cups and bowls are manufactured, but any experience with pressing and molding shapes into soft substances which can harden will create an analogy to some manufacturing processes. Thumbprint cookies, handprints in a plaster-of-paris filled plastic lid, a design-stamped butter pat, many of the operations children do with clay or play dough, footprints in the garden are all analogies to the way some products are formed.

You cannot quickly show children how stones become smooth and round. But you could give each child his or her own small new bar of soap (and a plastic lid with the child's name for a soap dish). Encourage observation of the wearing away of the writing and the rounding of shape as the bar is used through several days of hand washing. To secure the analogy, display a chunk of rock (granite, for example) and a smoothed stone or beach pebble of the same kind. Go to a beach and watch pebbles tumble in the waves at the edge of the water. Helping children to determine the ways two situations (the bar of soap, the piece of granite) are alike and different will aid understanding of analogous experiences in general.

Some analogies do not work well or in the interest of enlightenment. Sometimes we set up misunderstanding and do not know it, because we encourage analogous thinking without looking at differences. A common pitfall, for example, is putting human role expectations into our understanding of other animals. I read recently that an earthworm can be both "a father and a mother." It is true that earthworms are hermaphroditic, that is, each individual worm has both male and female reproductive functions—although another individual is required for reproduction. But "mother" and "father" they are not—in any combination.

Also, rodents of both sexes sometimes eat their young, not exactly a nurturant parental act. Yet most teachers insist on referring to these pets as the "mother hamster," the "father mouse," and so forth. Parents of many animal species would have to be described in the human social terms of this culture as poor providers, deserters, or energetic philanderers. If we insist on drawing improper or illogical analogies between human cultural roles and the biologically directed behavior of other species, we will be in the unscientific position of avoiding embarrassing questions or giving insensitive answers.

Other Vicarious Experiences.   Along with direct experience and vicarious or once-removed activities such as looking at pictures of phenomena, watching teacher demonstrations, or listening to stories, descriptions, and recordings, we can use analogies to bring meaning. Be aware of what you are doing. Stop and think about how often you expect children to understand a phenomenon on the basis of having experienced something *else*. Does the vicarious experience of analogy make sense? What are children likely to infer when they observe similarities? Differences? What conclusions are they likely to draw? If you want to increase a child's development of logical thinking, attention to these questions when you plan science experiences will help.

You Fit It All Together

Teachers guide science learning in many and diverse ways. Early childhood persons, perhaps because they consider development so carefully and plan for individual learning in each child, are good curriculum integraters. How does science work in? A satisfying science experience in a child's day may be sufficient just the way it is. It contributes to a child's life. However, teachers usually plan a follow-up or an expansion of a single science experience (or any other educational happening) for children. That's our job. It becomes a habit of thinking. Shall I supplement it? Build on it? Encourage its extension? When we are out in the yard with children, we find a nesting bird. We ask ourselves:

What else does/can this experience relate to? *How does an experience become a "topic"?* Where might the topic carry us? Into what other experiences, materials, topics? How many different directions might it go? How many can I anticipate, knowing this group of children? Stop right here—and come up with your own answers for the nesting bird. List them so you can deal with them some more. Then, see if they fit into one or more of the following groups.

Ways Experiences Relate

1. *Activities to pursue specific knowledge of this particular experience:* What kind of bird is it? What kind of nest did it make? How? Are both female and male parents around? Can we locate them? Observe differences and similarities in them. Observe the nesting habitat (is this a usual location, season, etc.?). What do they eat? One problem is that children will have to take it on faith that eggs are there. The nesting bird should not be disturbed. How can you maintain reverence for life and still supplement faith? Who has pertinent past experiences to share? What does the book say?

2. *Activities through time:* all of the above, plus watching for changes over days and weeks, thinking about last year and next. Many small touches provide continuity over time. Make sure the experience, or a similar one, is available again tomorrow. Set out the same equipment, perhaps with a small addition (Hawkins 1969). Daily recording or a diary of observations might be made with the group; older children may do their own with words or pictures. Make a photo study. Take the time to pursue information from reference sources. For the bird nesting, anticipate hatching, speculate, predict, and record predictions of children on number of days to hatch, number of young, appearance of young. What do the eggs look like? A book may tell you; later you can confirm by shell bits found on the ground maybe. Children wait to see; hopefully their patience will be rewarded with joyous witness to hatching and arduous nurturing and training of young birds.

3. *Activities which relate this experience to the overall curriculum experiences:* How can this experience be broadened to touch and intertwine with language development, music, motor activities, creative art, drama, and even snacktime? Do you have puppets that fit the topic? Can you get out a flannel board and parallel your daily observations with a story you and the children make? Do you have some appropriate books, pictures, songs, fingerplays, and art activities which will *add* to a child's understanding of, in this case, the avian life cycle? (For example *Baltimore Orioles* by Barbara Brenner.) Do the children's play, questions, and contributions to discussion give you some clues of where to go next with the topic? Have you ever tried weaving and daubing a model of a bird's nest with children? One big enough for children to get into?

4. *Activities which integrate science concepts with one another to build a general rational knowledge:* You pull out an old nest that fell from a tree last year, bits of bird's egg shells, or whatever you have in your cupboard. You plan walks to different kinds of environments where birds live—the park, the alley. You help

How can an experience be broadened to touch and intertwine with overall curriculum experiences? Do you have some appropriate books which will add to the child's understanding?

observations focus on birds, especially looking for the process of nest-building, since your group missed that part of the current sequence in your yard. You look for different kinds of birds and nests. You bring caged birds in, a mating pair of doves, for example (and good luck). You focus on many kinds of eggs—there are many pretty eggs all around the world, too. You see how different birds and other creatures have and rear young. You may get into incubation and hatching of chickens or ducks. You could focus on proper habitats and their attributes. You could explore food-getting, methods of feeding young, food chains, natural balances and how birds contribute, or other ecology studies of many kinds. You could center your concentration on building techniques, the use of dried grasses, twigs, feathers, human garbage, or whatever the children and experience suggest. You look at the activities of weaving, intertwining, stuffing, mud or clay stucco work—whatever the experience suggests. How do other species build shelters, if they do? In this particular geographical area? What other kinds of animals nest? What are the differences? Can we figure out some of the general needs of young creatures? How do life cycles of different kinds of creatures compare? What does it have to do with seasonal changes we are observing? Does this always hold true of birds? Only birds?

5. *Activities which relate this experience to the child's own self and life and lifestyle, and which integrate the experience with her or his experiences at home, in school, and in the child's culture and community:* Most children will feel a close affiliation with those potential young birds. Parents can share the news of what is happening at the center, and the other way around. Because this

example is about parenting, home ties to the experience will be especially close. A teacher might be particularly sensitive to avoiding a false analogy; therefore differences as well as similarities between birds and humans would be significant. Humans live in their shelter for many purposes. Human rearing is not seasonal; life span differences are great. Family configurations may or may not be the same. Do birds have grandmothers? We all participate in food chains, but the chains differ. Young have to be cared for in both forms of life, but not all forms of life need nurture from others after birth.

All of the points made and questions raised under the four groups above also contribute to the relationships and integration of knowledge here under group five. This is the most intensely personal, and at the same time the most expansively universal part of planning and teaching a science topic. Eventually you want the relationships of all forms of animal life to one another, and to the plants and other phenomena of the earth, to make sense. It does all fit together.

TEACHERS PROTECT CHILDREN AND OTHERS

The health and safety of children should be paramount considerations for all areas of curriculum. There are some special concerns in science. Why? Science is contact with and manipulation of the earth's phenomena. That can be really risky as well as threatening. *It is up to us to practice and preach intelligent caution and still encourage venturesome investigation.*

Intelligent caution is based on knowledge not ignorance. The governing rule is: The teacher should always know and understand what is going on. We have to know "What will happen if . . .?" Usually, we try a particular activity or check it out ahead of time. We know how to use the equipment before we get it out for children. We learn about it first. If we are uncertain, we investigate it. We eliminate hazards if possible. We seriously and firmly teach avoidance of those that cannot be eliminated. We help children learn, understand, and observe cautions as sensible behavior. We only undertake what we ourselves are comfortable about. And we expand our sense of comfort as we ourselves learn. All safety and health concerns have scientific bases. When we teach caution, we should be teaching science at the same time. We should know the reasons for concern and help children understand caution as rational behavior.

You Spot the Hazards

Look around your room. Take a trip through the building from the point of entry. Walk around your outdoor spaces. Look at patterns of walking and vehicle traffic and parking. Think about dangers in your furnishings, equipment, and facilities. Seek them out. List them. Decide how to cope with them and do it. Do this for every field trip and for every science experience. As you plan science, be aware of dangerous aspects of heat sources, animals, plants, machines, etc.

You Make the Rules

Children can help, too, because they are sometimes expert at hazard-coping. Rules that keep children safe are the best kind. Science safety, as for any other group activities, requires limitations on noise, size of the crowd, pace of activities. People cannot be allowed to push, throw materials, or hurt others. In science activities you may decide on special rules. Only adults plug in a lamp or appliance. Children who cut with the knife do it only on a cutting board, keeping both hands behind the blade, working individually, in a space away from others, using a motion away from their own bodies—and not at all until you can give them your undivided attention. Anyone using a rake or hoe in the garden must remember to rest it by sinking the head, the sharp edges or prongs, down into the ground. Everyone washes hands with soap before eating. Some rules for equipment safety are also suggested by Colton and Richtmyer (1975).

Children change. Some rules should flex developmentally, too. Maybe last fall you did not do much cooking at your center—children were too young. They reach the table surfaces better this spring, so that they have a safer angle on stirring hot pudding or slicing carrots. They learn to handle riskier situations as they grow. Help them learn gradually what is sensible and responsible. Help them gain skills with tools as they learn to use them safely.

Make rules which are sound. Make sure children understand and observe them. You will have to be the judge of what is appropriate for your setting and the children you know.

You Plan and Use Safe Materials and Experiences

You know about using nontoxic or nonpoisonous colors, paints, inks, and food coloring. You are sure the paint on your walls, furniture, and trays is not lead-based paint. You use blunt-ended scissors and needles. You put special equipment into adult-access-only storage which is locked or in a room not used by children. You keep cleaning supplies and household chemicals out of reach. You use utensils and containers made of glass only with special caution, when an adult is near, when children are in small quiet groups, or only for "looking." Glass utensils can serve your purpose so well that they are worth the trouble—glass makes a great aquarium. Like most substances, glass is safe if properly handled. But plastic or metal containers and utensils should be provided for children's general use. Make sure the edges of such tools are not cutting sharp or ripped. Supervise children's use of plastic wrap, sheeting, tablecloths, and bags carefully. Children can use small plastic bags, but to be safe, do not offer them any large enough to go over their heads. Keep plastics in adult storage areas. Watch for protruding nails, screws, and boards, and check play equipment for sharp edges, slivers, and rust spots where tears in metal develop easily. Also:

Guard heat sources, even radiators, and supervise anything hot.

Closely supervise ponds, pools, and tubs of water.

Provide safety goggles (just as you provide aprons or smocks to catch splashes) if you decide children are mature enough to use a rock pick, smash sugar cubes with a hammer, or pry into soft wood.

Encourage educated smelling—it is a good survival technique. But help children learn to approach the first whiff of anything with caution. Sharp smells or caustic substances, such as ammonia, can hurt the membranes inside the nose. Inhaling a substance through either nose or mouth is very dangerous. Make sure all "smelling jars" are tall cylinders (a paper roll with one end sealed will do) with the substance sample too far down to be drawn up by the whiff of an energetic young sniffer. Children can learn not to smell a moldy surface, soap suds, or whipped topping with noses too close. Learning how to cope with powders, fluffs, and finely chopped, dried, or mashed things can result from these cautions.

Children should not fear molds or fungi. They should investigate, learn, and appreciate the important biological functions of these decomposers. But they should not eat them or anything on which they grow, or handle them with bare hands. Mushrooms bought at the store and blue cheese are exceptions to the rule. Until *you* can tell the differences between harmless molds and very dangerous *Aspergillus fumigatus*, for example, or between an edible mushroom and deadly amanita, you better use tongs for handling. Wash hands carefully after handling. These precautions help children learn that people do not have to be irrational about dangerous, or possibly dangerous, substances—just smart.

Know which berries or leaves or roots are edible, out in the woods and in your garden. Until you can teach a child this knowledge, the child must learn to eat only food that is commercially obtained.

You should teach a child to inspect by looking and smelling and to make a sensible human judgment about grocery store food, too. Careful food selection could accompany interests in cooking and shopping. The conditions which can affect food quality are part of the scope of your science curriculum. The study of ripening, decomposition, and formation of gases as chemistry changes in food is most significant if you are about to put that food into your mouth.

Foods adults find perfectly acceptable may need to be introduced slowly to children. Pumpkin seeds or sunflower seeds, for example, can be shelled, roasted, and eaten with or without salt. They are nutritious snacks, and very high in fiber. Therefore, they, and similar high fiber foods, can badly affect a young digestive system not accustomed to such foods. Although a common accompaniment to carving the Halloween pumpkin at school is to roast the seeds, young children may be better off eating the pumpkin.

Popping and eating popcorn is a popular activity with American children of all ages. It is used as a preschool science activity. Dentists shudder; young teeth have a hard time chewing it, and nondigestible parts get stuck in teeth often not carefully cleaned. Because popcorn is morsel-sized, very dry, fibrous, and usually incompletely chewed, children can choke on it (and similar foods) easily. It is most often served in an activity or party atmosphere, increasing the likelihood of giggling and talking—hence choking—while eating.

Plan carefully the settings in which easy-choke foods are served or do not serve them. Teach children to separate eating and other oral activities. Talking with one's mouth full is not only unsavory to manner-conscious adults; it can also be fatal. Both are good reasons children should learn this caution.

You should know about special health needs of individual children. Substances easily handled, breathed, or eaten by almost everyone can trigger asthma, allergies, and other discomforts or illness in a few.

Wild animals should not be handled. If they let you approach very close, there may be something the matter. Sick animals may even approach you, but leave them alone. Help children learn to look and enjoy the sight of all animals but touch only creatures they know are safe.

Children can learn to approach any and all domestic animals and other people's pets to whom they are strangers with caution—not fear. The more you know about these animals, the more you can help children learn.

Check any pet carefully. Obtain it from a reliable source. When in doubt about the condition of an animal, check with a veterinarian. A few birds have the disease psittacosis, and it can be a serious condition in humans. Parrots and parakeets are likely sources. Turtles from the pet store have been so likely to carry salmonellosis, a bacterial infection, that sale of these pets has been banned in some places. Turtles from your local pond may also be infected. Leave them there. If you think turtles are important, or you already have some, check with a veterinarian about ongoing prevention and treatment of salmonellosis.

Several kinds of salmonella bacteria can cause serious salmonellosis ("food infections") in young children. Sick dogs are occasionally infected and can infect children. Be especially careful of any animal with diarrhea. A more likely and threatening source is dried eggs. Anything made with dried eggs (including cake mixes and other prepackaged batter and dough mixes) may be a source of trouble. Dried eggs can certainly be used in your cooking, but all foods prepared with them should be thoroughly cooked or baked. Children should not eat any *raw* batter containing dried eggs—no licking the pan. With babies and toddlers, salmonellosis is a special threat because they are liable to put contaminated objects into their mouths or eat things older persons would not find palatable and because salmonellosis often makes young children especially ill.

Some plants commonly found indoors or out, in various parts of the country, are poisonous. Some may be fatal to a child who eats even very small amounts. Teachers must learn about and recognize these killers, which can be found in parks, schoolrooms, and yards, as well as in woods and swamps. Children must be cautioned early not to put unknown plants into their mouths.

Although much is still unknown about poisonous plants, the appendix to this book (p. 119) provides a guide to some that cause the most trouble. The appendix does not include treatment for poisoning because the best advice is to call a doctor or your local poison control center. Vomiting should not be induced at home until so advised by the doctor, since a few extremely strong plant poisons can add to irritation or burning of weakened digestive tract tissue as they are regurgitated. For more complete information on prevention and treatment, identification charts, and guidance on inservice training in this area, contact your state department of health, your local U.S. Department of Agriculture extension agent, or write: National Safety Council, 425 N. Michigan Avenue, Chicago, IL 60611.

Noise can be harmful. Young children's centers can be too noisy for health —auditory or psychological. If a child complains of specific noise, listen to what she or he is telling you. The child may hear to the point of distress something you barely perceive. Your quieting cautions are much appreciated. Use carpeting, padding, and techniques which slow down or quiet the activity pace of the group if it is too much. Eliminate some sounds when noise peaks. Background music can be pleasant, but it can also add to the amount of noise (Pitts 1975d).

Mosquitoes, houseflies, and cockroaches are a lot more dangerous—because of the diseases and infections they may carry—than are many of the insects which are more likely to panic teachers, such as beetles and their larvae, or bumblebees. Knowing about insects is worthwhile. Children can find a fascinating chapter of life under a log. We may join many cultures in the world who use insects as an accessible and very edible source of protein—it may not appeal to you, but teach children to respect and know bugs. As children learn about insects, they should be cautious about dangerous ones and respectful of all of them.

Spiders are not insects. A very few of them are poisonous and some bite. Check with your own area for local knowledge. Spiders are fascinating; do not discourage interest in them.

TEACHERS LEARN

If you persist in doing right by children, and if I have not lost you already, you may be feeling some new needs. The best model for a learning child is a learning adult. "But *science*? . . . Me?" Yes, that is the nice thing about it. No one ever knows it all. The processes of science are learning processes for all of us.

You Use Community Resources

Where do you go to find out? If you live in an urban place, you have access to museums and zoos. Such places are staffed by people who can help you find answers. You may have to ask. The public library will help you, even over the telephone or by your placing an order through the mobile library services. A librarian can often help find exactly the right picture of a scorpion, a seahorse, or a sand dune. Library staff can show you where to browse among books about making windmills. Children's librarians know their selections well. They can help you find a children's book about rock formations or pulleys.

You might try the cooperative extension service (U.S. Department of Agriculture) in your county, whether your setting is rural or not. Extension publications can help you learn to do many things, indoor and outdoor gardening, for example. If you do your business by mail, write the state cooperative extension service office at your land grant university. Public Health services, state or local, are good places to get safety, health, and nutrition aids and information too.

Don't overlook the field offices of other government services. Forest Service (U.S. Department of Agriculture) personnel, Fish and Wildlife Service (U.S. Department of Interior), or conservation commission, or whatever your state or county offices are called, are good resources. Public education is an increasing part of the job of these government services. The natural resources they manage and protect will fare better at the hands of an informed public. Usually the staff people are eager to be a part of any science education endeavor. Locally, look to your park supervisor's office. You can tap into the county or city architect or engineer's office. Sometimes design, engineering, and construction questions can open a new area of applied science for the young children you work with, too. Your money pays these people. Don't hesitate to ask public employees for help.

Among private groups, you can sometimes find help from industries who have special sensitivity to educational benefits. Farm organizations can be helpful, especially locally. You know that some local establishments delight in hosting you and children when you visit on a field trip. Many business people can also help you learn. A junkyard dealer knows about different kinds of metal, how to tell them apart, separate them, what their properties are, or what they are used for, and he or she is a good resource for equipment too. A food cooperative or health food store may be your best resource for seeing, procuring, and learning to use a variety of raw whole grains and legumes. Such a place would make a good field trip site.

You Help Each Other

When you are listing your community sources, don't overlook your friends. Adults learn from each other. Parents and teachers learn from one another; teachers learn from other teachers, parents learn from other parents. Sharing your interests and activities in science can uncover some new resources for everyone. You might even form an interest group with regular meetings. Older children and teenagers are often walking storehouses of science experiences; they have studied it more recently, and maybe differently, than we have. Our parents and grandparents learned it in still different ways, often firsthand. It is the blight of our ageism prejudices that we often believe we can learn best from someone older, but not much older. Children would be the winners if we could pass on a good feeling for the *accumulation of wisdom from each life's experience which makes up science for us all.*

Marty's grandpa settled himself down among the children at the day care center.

"When I was a boy," he began, "not much bigger than some of you, I went with my dad to my first big shearing." As he talked of this task, and the years of ranch life, the children gathered closer, asking about the sheep and examining the raw wool and tools he brought. He told of the habits of sheep and their great need for care. The heavy smell of the wool, the clean greasy feel of it, and the old wool grower's skillful pantomime and sparkling descriptions of those days made us believe we were there. As he laughed, "You'll never see a shearer with dry, chapped hands," we all looked down at our hands, rubbing our fingers together, feeling the lanolin residue. It made sense.

You Organize Inservice Training

No one knows what you want to learn better than you. Getting training of any kind is very difficult for many in full-time centers, on small budgets, or in isolated areas. Getting the training we need is hard for everyone. Sometimes you have to group together. Do you have input into program planning for professional meetings? Can you submit your suggestions to your director? Can you organize a series of presentations to a group? Can you ask your state office of child development for help? (Do you have one?) How about talking it over with your local college or vocational short-course planners? Some topics of information are easier to acquire in groups. Groups of teachers, groups of parents, or, stronger yet, groups of parents and teachers together—you work with the same children. If you get together and state what you want to learn, you can often get help through your area education agency. Go to the high school and ask how to proceed from there.

Because you are the one who knows what you need to know, I cannot suggest many topics. Start a list, and begin talking with your science-needing colleagues. To get your discussion started, Table 3 lists a few topics I bet you have never asked for before. Are you intrigued?

Table 3. Inservice Training Sessions You Have Always Wanted but Were Afraid to Ask For

A. The Ecology Series
1. The ecology of our playground: "What do you call *that*, Teacher?"
2. The ecology of our alley: rocks in our road and other phenomena.
3. The ecology of our neighborhood park: the flora and fauna of city park #2.
4. The ecology of our vacant lot: life under the litter.
5. The ecology of our guppy tank: food chains, air tubes, and other lifelines.

B. The Curriculum Integration Series
1. The edible curriculum: how to spend your science education budget on food, or vice versa.
2. Creative crafts chemistry: colors, bonds, and wrinkles with natural inedibles.
3. Playground physics: how to tell a swinging gate from a centrifuge.
4. The metric system: a human awareness clinic.
5. City planning and curriculum integration: an analogy.

C. **Knowing to Learn; Learning to Know Series**
   1. Dinosaurs, fossils, and other dug treasures.
   2. To dissect or not to dissect? That is a several-edged question.
   3. How a building is put together.
   4. The working ways of a furnace, featuring also where telephone lines are and how to read the gas meter.
   5. Group discipline and management: ants, bees, and day care centers do it.

You Set Up a Teacher's Resource Center

Whether at home or at school, you are at an advantage if you have a few resource books handy. I have referred to a few examples. Most of these, because they are good resources, lead you to their lists of other resources. You may not be able to provide all of these for your own center, but, over time, you might collect a few which suit your needs best. If your local public library does not have some of them, request their purchase; they are useful to parents and teachers.

1. General Sourcebooks. I recommended four: Hone, Joseph, and Victor (1962); Finch (1971); UNESCO (1962); and Pavoni, Hagerty, and Heer (1974). There are many more. Pavoni et al. is an environmental reference, written for teachers, which explains the scientific aspects of ecological and environmental issues. Curriculum suggestions for older beginning and advanced students are given. The other three books are general, covering children's traditional science topics, biological and physical. They deal with such items as how clouds are formed, what to do for a tadpole, the difference between charcoal and coal—things you would be more comfortable with if you knew. These books give the adult facts currently known on a topic, plus suggestions for activities for children. Any one of these is a good place to start for "I don't know. Let's look it up" activities. Hone et al. (1962) and Finch (1971) especially are the places for common science questions. UNESCO (1962) is rich in suggestions for fashioning equipment.

2. Topical Sourcebooks. There are many, many of these, especially for nature studies. Each one is on a different topic. Most are very well illustrated, making them good sources for pictures, too. You may be familiar with the Golden Nature Guides written by Herbert S. Zim and associates. These paperbook books are readily available on bookstands. Each guide presents color illustrations and brief information on the given topic. While not adequate for the advanced student, the books include most common species (or whatever the specific volume is about) in this country, for example Zim (1955).

The Peterson Field Guide series, now numbering 21 titles, is a detailed set of identification sourcebooks covering most aspects of nature study: seashells, butterflies, reptiles and amphibians, wildflowers, stars and planets, mammals, insects, ferns, trees and shrubs, rocks and minerals. There are five bird books (for example, *A Field Guide to Western Birds* 1961) and several records of bird songs in the series.

Museums and nature associations frequently have either their own or other topic related publications. The American Museum of Natural History (Central Park West at 79th Street, New York, NY 10024) publishes *Natural History* magazine and occasionally makes nature topic paperback books available (Vroman 1967, for example). Look also to the National Audubon Society (950 Third Avenue, New York, NY 10022) magazine, *Audubon,* and the National Wildlife Federation (1412 16th Street, Washington, DC 20036) publications, *Conservation News, Ranger Rick's Nature Magazine,* and *National Wildlife Magazine.* These publications are also good sources of photographs and drawings of superb quality.

Because any sourcebooks of nature would be most useful to you if they pertained to your own area, see if you can find a local source. A museum of natural history, a museum of science and technology, a state museum, a city museum, or a museum of regional interest would be good sources for you to investigate. The British Columbia Provincial Museum, for example, currently has some 27 titles in print on the plants, animals, and habitats of British Columbia (Carl 1971). These regional museums, besides offering rich displays, often can recommend books, records, and films of your area's natural phenomena.

You should become acquainted with a resource lover's resource, *Environmental Education: A Guide to Informational Sources,* by Stapp and Liston (1975). This publication is part of an environment information guide series. In it, you will find annotated lists of names, addresses, and brief descriptions of

instructional aids, reference materials, government services, organizations
and associations, periodicals, preservice and inservice education programs
and centers, funding sources—all these refer to environmental education.
Many sources of catalogues and free or free-loan materials are cited.

3. Activities Sourcebooks. Some sources which give you many suggestions
of appropriate science activities on varied topics for *young* children are: Austin
Association for the Education of Young Children (1973), Baker (1966), Bender
(1969), Carmichael (1969), Gordon-Nourok (1975), Hucklesby (1971), Ovitt
(1966), and Pitts (1971-1975). Most general textbooks in early childhood education have sections on science curriculum and its facilitation. Journals and
newsletters in the field frequently carry science-related articles.

You Adapt Resources

There are not very many science resources for use with young children. The
examples suggested for activities may be too complex, or in some way not
right, for the very young or very inexperienced or restricted children you
know. That's where you come in. You will find, too, some resources give ideas
which do not fit your geography, your season, or your budget. You devise. You
can find an abundance of activities and curriculum aids for elementary
schools. At these age levels, there are elaborate grade-age sets and materials. If
you have access to these use them by all means. But use them in ways you know
best with young children. Some adult resources, as I have pointed out, offer
beautiful materials. You must fashion the fit.

Many science activities books are written for parents and teachers of older
children. I have used two that are especially adaptable: *Guppies, Bubbles, and
Vibrating Objects* by McGavack and LaSalle (1969) and *Teaching Science with
Everyday Things* by Schmidt and Rockcastle (1968). Both of these are based on
unit approaches to teacher-defined, content-oriented objectives. That is not
where science should start for younger children. However, many of the actual
experiences are simple and direct—and discoverable. They also confine themselves to simple, inexpensive equipment most of us can obtain.

Perhaps the richest sources of materials to adapt for young children are
books written for older children. Check the science shelves in the children's
area of your public library. If you want answers, it is a good place to find
accurate, simple, well-illustrated information. You cannot read these books to
young children; it would turn them off. You have to tell the messages and
information in words your children will understand. Here, for example, are
seven such books.

A Zoo in Your Room, by Roger Caras
Night Animals, by Daniel Cohen
The Blossom on the Bough: A Book of Trees, by Anne O. Dowden
Science Fun with a Flashlight, by Herman and Nina Schneider
Gerbils and Other Small Pets, by Dorothy Shuttlesworth
Guinea Pigs: All about Them, by Alvin and Virginia Silverstein
The Story of Your Skin, by Edith Lucie Weart

Some of these authors have written other science books for children. Your librarian can help you find additional books on topics from prehistoric life to advances in human medicine.

You are the person between children and materials which were not designed with them particularly in mind. Only the materials you design have that advantage. You are the one who knows your children. You know each child. *You must always adapt for individuals, no matter how developmentally appropriate the materials.* Making a good match between this child and an array of appropriate activities is what you know more about than anyone or any book or any set of curriculum materials. When you personalize, adapt, and make a good match, you are the *teacher.*

TEACHERS FEEL, BELIEVE, AND ARE

The days filled with children and learning and science are exciting days. They should give you self-satisfaction. The feelings and attitudes teachers have, the thoughts and truths they accept and believe, and the persons they are—these are important in the science they do with young children. Adults figure into nearly everything young children do when they are with us, whether we are trying to or not. We "teach" them what we are by being.

You Regard Yourself

Highly, I hope. I have already mentioned some ways teachers can take stock and appreciate what they do with children. You are the assessor of your own needs, your own knowledge, your own learning and growing, your own expanding comfort with science and with children. As you look at yourself and science, become more aware of your strengths. You may honestly find some areas within you that need work, too. Do you have some hang-ups, some barriers within yourself which might affect the learning opportunities you arrange—or avoid—for children? Some attitudes in adults can certainly stop or slow down children's science inquiries. Very few young children have these obstacles in their heads. Far too many teachers do—and they can be contagious attitudes which ought to be classified as *dangerous contaminants* of effective science education.

Beware of Dangerous Contaminants

Let's examine some of the attitudes we are talking about.

Sexism in Science. We should be very sensitive to establishing a nonsexist science approach for young children. Be sure all children have equal access to the science experiences you plan and provide. Encourage scientific inquiry in all children. Assume children of both sexes will be interested and ready, and that individual interests will not vary by sex. Also, see Sprung (1975) and check to see how your "hidden messages" transmit.

But it is more than possible that people all along the line did not give you

the same chances. If you are a woman, you may have found the biggest part of the answer to the question, "Why is science our worst area?" You may be afraid of science. Unless your own childhood experiences were truly exceptional, you were given a heavy dose of the sexist message: Women can know a little about science, but only men do it. So maybe you learned a little of the "what," although not much. You may have been told in hundreds of variations through your growing up that science was not for girls. At best, you might have heard of Madame Curie, the token woman in the history of science. But you never learned the "how" at all.

Fear is based, in this case, on ignorance of what scientific experimentation means and of how to build it, fix it, rig it, test it, and make it work. And even if you can do all those things, can you take full credit for it? Can you be proud and satisfied without the slightest hint of feeling that you have done something not quite proper? Can you talk about it comfortably—to anyone? Or do you hide behind the ignorance that sexism builds? It is *so* easy to let Bill do it. And you do know how to get him to do it—that you were taught. Because you learned to behave in certain "feminine" ways, you may now find you have some specific obstacles to overcome, too—your feelings about snakes, for example, or is it mice?

If you are a man, you may have another kind of problem. You, too, do not wish to be the model fulfillment of a sexist upbringing. You want to do right by children, all children. You will note the curriculum comments later suggest the best science with young children deals with the phenomena closest to them—their bodies, their food, and their clothing. No formaldehyde. No electrical transformer. Just the stuff of life. The only trouble is, you were raised to feel these bread-and-shirts issues were of a woman's world. Sexism strikes again. You also may feel you have to prove a great deal more than the wisdom of the scientific method. You may have to be right. The association of authority with masculinity is our social heritage. Your struggle with yourself may be in assuming an open mind, in learning to be flexible, and in letting a little child lead you.

Some Specific Nature Hang-Ups.   Most of these are directly related to sexism. Some are more likely to be associated with certain subgroups of sex, age, and culture than others. I have already mentioned some. Can you think of any others?

Snakes.   Persons who live in areas of the country also populated by copperhead, water moccasins, coral, or rattlesnakes can tell you why they are wary of these snakes. Their cautions support survival. People under these conditions learn to identify harmful snakes, know their habits and haunts, and work out ways of avoiding the snakes and protecting themselves. These people cope well with a hazard and usually teach children to do so. A city dweller who sees a curved stick in the grass of the park and screams hysterically does not

Children should learn respect for all forms of life and should know which forms are congenial and which would threaten a human life if disturbed.

cope well with danger. Once again knowledge makes for more sensible behavior then ignorance. Certainly a shudder and groan when the word *snake* is mentioned is a habit society should no longer reward. Children should learn respect for all forms of life and should know which forms are congenial and which would threaten a human life if disturbed. *Animals That Frighten People*, by Dorothy E. Shuttlesworth, is a children's book which discusses snakes, bats, spiders, and a few others; it is a good resource for this topic.

Rodents. Much of the same is true here. Children need cautions about rats. Rats, especially Norway or brown rats, can be a threat to humans wherever they abound. They carry serious diseases. You may know this only too well, and not really feel comfortable with rats in your classroom, even if they are special pets in a cage. O.K. Trust yourself. It makes sense. But don't generalize to gerbils, hamsters, or guinea pigs. Even mice are more nuisance than threat. It has been pointed out that if humans ate milkweed, monarch butterflies would be the enemy, too. Many creatures we have learned to fear are actually competitors for our food supply, and that is the threat. An adult's aversion to all small, furry things will not serve science well. Besides, young children really like them. Our battle should be with the sentimentalizing of these natural phenomena in children's literature and goods—that is not scientific, either. The realities of these forms of life are more exciting.

Insects.   Again, here is an example where aversion to experience and knowledge runs high among adults. Being able to identify the harmful bugs in your geographic area is important; children should know this and should check with a knowledgeable adult before they approach insects or spiders. Bugs provide nature study for everyone. No matter what your setting, you will find them.

Enclosing a small area—the area inside a tire, a plastic hoop, or a circle of rope or tapeline, for example, gives you and children a defined piece of earth to study (McIntyre 1975d). Chances are it will contain insects of several kinds. Cracks in walls and sidewalks can be rich too. You can help children begin to have respect for the important functions insects have in our own lives—plant pollination, balance in insect populations and biotic communities, soil manipulations and enrichments, etc.

Slime, slush, and softness.   Ever stop to assess your own preferences for textures? Or how you acquired them? The soft, wet, slimy creatures of the earth rarely are teachers' favorites, thus avoidance of some fascinating forms of life can be passed from one generation to another. I have seen zealous ten-year-olds stamping out the lives of slugs, grubs, and larvae as if ridding the world of a great scourge. They do not treat wildflowers or beetles that way. How did they learn the difference? As with all forms of life, some of these creatures are more congenial to human priorities and purposes than others. All of them, however, play a part in the ecology of their area. All of them, from a scientific point of view, should be acceptable subjects for study. None should be mindlessly destroyed because of their textures. If a gardener destroys slugs, there should be recognition that another value system is coming into play— one in which technology plays some part—but it is not by all standards scientific. It is a value and a choice.

Worms.   "Here, Teacher. Hold my worm—*careful.*" And there you are, ready or not. Are you ready? And are you enormously respectful? Earthworms are doing more than their share of the world's work. Like insects, their processing of soil leaves it richer by far. The holes and burrows and bumps they make allow water to distribute through the soil—although they make a second-rate suburban lawn. If you define the tickle and scrunch in your hand as a "bad" feeling, look back and see where you acquired the psychological burden.

Decomposition and putrefaction.   Do the words themselves start you churning? You can almost smell it now! That's one way we know enough not to eat it. Generally, people are likely to leave such things alone. It is a good message— the bacteria and fungi do not need any help. But aversive attitudes can be overstated. Children can easily get the idea that decomposition is bad. However, these processes are just as important in natural production as budding and ripening. And, if anything, they are more interesting. Children are drawn to decaying wood or a dead rabbit. Don't draw them away. They should not touch an animal's carcass as a rule. Protect them from what may be unsafe. But do not protect them from knowledge. A squirrel which has been run over in the street can afford city children a rare opportunity to see "insides"—use the opportunity.

Propriety.   We grew up with feelings for rules, standards, or a decorum which may have served us well. We can also catch ourselves, especially in science, having many reactions based on a code we learned when we were children. We have to examine our proprieties and see if they still make sense—especially in light of ever increasing scientific knowledge and much greater environmental awareness, not to mention our increasing maturity. For example, many of us learned the hard way not to pick grandma's garden flowers, but that wildflowers existed for little hands to uproot at will. That is a propriety. I strongly suggest that you teach and carry out a completely revised ethic: pick what you plant. Leave wild growth alone, especially in natural settings.

A related propriety is telling a young child, "Don't pick the lovely trillium, Carla. Let's leave it there for other people to enjoy." That may make the adult feel better, but it is not reasoning which is scientific or which teaches science. The primary reason to leave it alone is that it has a natural, biological function. Picking it interferes with that function—terminally. Nothing in nature is there solely for the purpose of giving human beings pleasure. Aesthetic benefits derived from other forms of life are beautiful, but incidental to the natural function of any life: to live and die in the style of its species. Any disturbance of one form of life can eventually make trouble for all forms.

Another propriety: Taking apart is destructiveness. As a science educator, you plant flowers for picking and for picking apart to see what is inside. When other uses are exhausted, the old clock will still be fascinating as a dissecting experience. So will your dead catfish.

Here is another propriety: Clutter is mess and mess is sloppy and sloppy is bad. Or another: Soil is dirt and dirt is filth and filth is bad. See how you can catch yourself in your own web of knowledge-dodging? Children do not benefit when adults live by old myths.

Inhibitions and Prohibitions.   These are proprieties, too, but deeper and more serious within us, therefore less open to examination, even our own. These may include reactions to the essences of life: sex, reproduction, birth, body parts, bodily processes, and death. To humans, these may well be the most important and highly valued of all scientific phenomena. They may also be most heavily laden with cumbersome bundles of conflicting values. Is that why we can often find them categorized in very unnatural cubbyholes of our minds? Is that why so many of us have a hard time dealing with questions about life's most wondrous aspects? Children want to know. These are the questions some of us do *not* encourage. Some of us seem to believe that children's curiosity is good *unless* it is about their own bodies, and we have discouraged learning through direct experience or any other way. Where are you?

Why is it so many of us have a hard time dealing with questions about life's most wondrous aspects?

What do you think is *best for the children* you teach? (I did not say "easiest for you.") You know where science stands, don't you?

> *The last jungles in the world seem to withdraw almost eagerly from advancing man. The forests drain themselves of beasts and flatten into meadows, the meadows are turned into suburbs, and the suburbs are swallowed by our cities. The only thriving wildlife still barely touched by man is the hot, confusing, and poorly lit world within himself. (Vroman 1967, p. ix)*

Thus begins an enlightening and entertaining book on one of the most inhibited of all topics—human blood, or, as Vroman calls it, "this alarming treasure." How do you react when a child cuts a finger? We have difficulty teaching others what we have not accepted. But if you understand and believe that pain and bleeding have positive survival functions, you can give these attitudes along with your first aid.

> Here, Jerry, let me see it. It's bleeding, good! That cleans it. Now I'm going to hold this clean gauze over your cut tightly. Do you feel how tight that is? . . . I'll bet it hurt, didn't it? . . . The hurt makes you do something quickly to take care of your body. And we're doing it. When we hold the bandage over the cut so tight, it gives your blood a chance to 'coagulate.' That means it gets thick and then stops flowing. That's how you start to heal and the cut gets better. Think that's long enough? O.K. Let's see. Good, now we'll use some of this medicine to clean away any outsiders: things like bacteria, maybe, that we couldn't even see. Inside your skin is always clean. Your blood does that. But when you get an opening in your skin, outside material can get in, even when the blood comes out and cleans the cut. That's why we clean your cut with this. There. You did well. Want a Band-Aid?

Bleeding, mucous, saliva, tears, perspiration, elimination of urine and feces—these physiological substances and functions are healthy and full of scientific wonder. Accepting them as such can do a great deal to enhance the spirit of a child as well as her or his intelligent mind. A happy self-feeling is strengthened by knowing and appreciating oneself inside as well as outside. Accepting oneself *totally*, with no exceptions or unmentionable parts or processes, is what a "healthy self-image" means. Sprung (1975) discusses nonsexist activities and resources for young children concerning human bodies. *Bodies* by Barbara Brenner (1973) is also a good book to use and enjoy with young children.

It would be a poor science program if it avoided the processes of life. Young children understand the beginnings of reasonable explanations when they want them and are ready. They seem to understand a great deal about adult attitudes long before that. Teachers can show uneasiness by answering too much as well as by avoiding questions (Elkind 1970). If you feel comfortable and accepting about sex and birth and death, you relax about these topics with children. You have to believe there will be a tomorrow. These, like all phenomena of the earth, seem best learned gradually over time, as understanding is built with maturity. That is why an all-the-time-and-wherever science approach is most sensible. Teachers have to be ready.

Your training helps. Seek it. Right now, death is a topic of wide humanistic interest. You may find discussion groups of persons helping themselves and each other toward greater ease and more understanding. Some teachers do not keep animals or fish in their classrooms because they are afraid of not being able to handle the death of a pet with children. There is material for both adults and children to help you with these topics in your science planning, for example, "Why Isn't the Gerbil Moving Anymore?" by G. P. Koocher (1975).

Early childhood teachers have been sensitive to the great interest young children have in reproduction. It is a developmentally appropriate, egocentric interest. Young children are physically small and close in time and spirit to their own infancies. They are intensely aware of babyhood in other creatures—it is still their era. Their parents usually are young adults who have young friends, so new babies among the social group are not uncommon events. It will be a regular occurrence among the families of children at an early childhood center. Wise teachers know this, and plan many events in their science curriculum which supplement comfort and knowledge. Live-bearing fish such as guppies, mollies, swordtails, or platys, or mammals such as rodents whose gestation period and growing-through-infancy development are relatively short in time, are favorite reproduction experiences. Wise teachers seek parent involvement in these and other aspects of curriculum development. Families who share these experiences often find the actual arrival of a new baby easier for parents and young children.

The real hang-up of some adults is a bone-chilling dread that some day some child will ask a human question on a human subject: "But Teacher, how did the baby get inside its mother?" It is an interesting superinhibition, from a nonsexist point of view. Males play a vital role in conception of all forms of new animal life; their nurturance of the conceived life then varies, as does the females' depending more or less on the biological dictates of the species. It is a crime against all humanity that boys should go through their formative years thinking only females have anything to do with reproduction—and that is happening, especially to urban children. Early childhood teachers should consider the prime importance of this piece of growing-up information for boys and girls both. There are three basic animal reproduction concepts, in fact, that even very young children can begin to grasp:

It takes two parents of the same animal species to produce normal offspring. (I say "normal" because there are a few animal species crosses—horse + donkey = mule is an example. But these creatures do not reproduce. Beefalo, buffalo-cattle crosses, allegedly do reproduce, but the conditions are still unknown and questionable.)

Prenatal arrangements and care vary greatly throughout the animal world. In nearly all mammals, including humans, the young grow from eggs fertilized within the female's body by the male and are born live.

Young animals, including humans, grow up to be like their parents: of the same species and with the same species characteristics. All humans are born of human parents and will have human characteristics.

An honest, scientific, and humane answer to the question above is, "The mother's body makes an egg and the father's body makes a sperm. The sperm joins the egg in the mother's body. The two cells grow together to make a new life"—or words to that effect. The topic is human conception. If discussing other species, avoid the social sex role trap and use the terms *male* and *female* for the hamsters and guppies. Now, if the topic is human sexual intercourse, then human love-making could be discussed. However, the topic is unlikely to be of major interest to young children unless it is part of the observation reality of their own lives. Should this be true, then wholesome, positive knowledge can help them handle that better than ignorance or lies or mythology or street talk, which is a combination of all four. The egocentrism of young children functions in such a way that they seem considerably more interested in their own origins than in the adult interests and motivations which produced them.

Your Strengths Count

You should count them dearly. These attitudes, feelings, and beliefs will do more for your science program than a triple budget.

Your Uniqueness.   Teachers are individuals too. Children can be worn down to boredom and routine functioning in a hurry if all teachers sound and act alike. Your own feelings, interests, and motivations should combine to assure that the way you do things is your very own.

Your Energy.   Shaping and setting up a program is hard work. Your willingness to put in the extra measure of verve necessary to locate materials, scrounge some equipment, or scout a field trip route is what makes a science program—packing it, unpacking it; getting it out, putting it away; borrowing it, returning it. These are *your* processes. They sometimes seem endless and mundane. Not so. These are teaching processes just as surely as your sensitive encouragement of budding intellect through discussion of experimental findings. Without teacher-work, at home or school, there will be no science program. You have to believe it is worth it.

Your Interests.   Your own curiosity and intellectual problem-solving approach is going to teach children. If you are an effective and persistent seeker of knowledge and an open-minded, flexible person, ready to follow a promising direction with children, you are a fine science model. Your careful observations, your thoughtful planning, require a mind set toward science. You think about science a lot, and about how to do it with children. You expand your own knowledge of resources and activities enthusiastically. You find joy in discovering the world with children. You look forward to it. You are also a model for how to handle frustrations and faulty experiments. You can admit your mistakes and learn from them with children. Truth really is more important than face-saving.

Your Coping with Problems.   You believe in the scientific method; you use it. You live it. Whether you are trying to figure out what is the matter with the radiator or why Samantha is so listless and quiet, you are problem solving. You are using scientific method. First, you observe carefully. (Samantha is sad or something this morning.) You repeat, you look again. (Samantha has hung up her coat and is wandering around, but not finding an activity.) You vary the conditions. (Samantha has seen her friends. Andrea has shouted to her to come over, but Samantha did not respond.) You compare instances to each other

and to knowns or experiences you have had in the past. (Samantha does not
seem interested in anything that is going on. Samantha is not usually like this.)
You hypothesize. (Samantha may be tired? Coming down with flu? Maybe
something happened at home?) You experiment. (Let's see if Samantha would
like to help make cookie dough.) You evaluate. (Samantha seems to be enjoying the activity vigorously.) You infer. (Samantha cannot be coming down
with the flu, she's too active now.) You draw conclusions. (Whatever was
wrong, Samantha seems like her usual self now.) You verify. (Samantha con-
tinues to enjoy her activities. Later, Samantha's grandmother tells you the
family was up late the night before and overslept, making a rushed morning
for everyone.) You know.

Your Involvement.   You believe that science is important, children are important, and you are important. You want to do a good job on behalf of children. It is more important than being an authority or having the right answer.
You look for ways to work better science with children. You really care, and
that is the greatest strength of all. You *do* believe it is worth it.

PERSONAL ECOLOGY:
THE CONTENT OF
YOUNG CHILDREN'S
SCIENCE

THE CONTENT OF YOUNG CHILDREN'S SCIENCE

Snowflakes drift.
I taste winter
melting on my lips. *

I have discussed science and its functions and have suggested children's attributes and activities, and many things teachers can do to guide children and science together. In other words, I have talked about "methods." But what about "content"? When you are planning science with young children, *what* do you intend to teach? *What* do you hope they learn?

THE TRADITIONS, THE PHENOMENA, AND THE MIDDLE PERSON

Traditions Are Adult-Oriented

What is your orientation to science? Are you thinking about children learning how to solve problems, discover things, and do activities to sense, manipulate, experiment, and find out? Or are you concerned about their learning facts as you learned them? The tradition in education has been the latter. Even early childhood educators have been known to state their science objectives in terms of the pieces of conglomerates of information they wish a child to acquire. But this mature orientation should be reserved for adults.

With an emphasis on science content and fact-learning comes a focus on traditional disciplines or areas: the biological sciences, the physical sciences and mathematics, the behavioral sciences. Or, people talk about the "pure" sciences (studying the basic phenomena) and the "applied" sciences (using scientific methods and findings of pure science to solve problems for humans). You are probably familiar with the traditional science fields such as physics, chemistry, bacteriology, botany, zoology, anthropology, human development, and on and on. These divisions of knowledge and endeavor are arbitrary and the fields overlap. They are handy, but they are for adults, too. When you try to give them equal time in your early childhood curriculum, you run into trouble.

The Phenomena Are for Everyone

Though the traditional science fields are for adults, the happenings of the earth are here for experiencing by everyone. Science also means encountering, discovering, and investigating these phenomena in an increasingly methodical and cumulative-constructive way. This has been done through history; the results which have built up are the adult sciences as we know them. We have emphasized the probing and finding because it is not only more developmentally basic but also more basic to science.

---

* Kazue Mizumura, *I See the Winds*, New York: Thomas Y. Crowell, 1966. Used by permission.

You Are the Middle Person

You stand between the great traditions of adult science and the great mysteries of young children's learning. You will not only guide the experiences; you will choose some of them. If it could be assumed that children would encounter the science they needed naturally, the job would be easy. But theirs is often not a natural world.

Science has to be (1) available, (2) appealing, and (3) appropriate in order for the child to get fully involved. I have discussed availability and appeal to some extent. What is appropriate? Let me restate and elaborate two of the sets of assumptions cited in the beginning of this book.

The most effective sources of early learning experiences are:

- Closest to the child. This means most immediate in time, nearest in actual physical proximity, and most similar in key attributes such as size, form, age, and culture.
- Of the child's own encounter, discovery, choice, and/or creation.
- Those which directly serve the child's own immediate needs.

Learning experiences should be planned to expand gradually through time and sequence, beginning from the child's own physical, social, intellectual, emotional, and spiritual self. Curricula content should therefore:

- Start with the child's body in motion—activities the child does and the child's actual sensory contact. Through time, and logical/developmental sequence, education experiences can gradually become more remote, farther away from the child's immediate experience and reality *but based on it.*
- Continually change, being based on developmental abilities, expanding interests, and accumulating experience of children.
- Vary with individual children at a given time.

THE CHILD AS A CENTER OF EXPERIENCE

Personal Ecology as a Science Framework

Ecology is the study of interrelations of living beings and things with the environments in which they exist. Under ecology quite properly go considerations of energy flows, of cycles and patterns among natural phenomena, of the stability or instability of natural systems, of populations and communities of all forms of life. Can you think of specific examples of ways all of these ideas relate to children? A child is in active interaction with the environment as a condition of growth. I have tried to center on the individual child. Therefore, I propose the concept of "personal ecology" as a guide to the science experiences you choose or focus on or uncover as your curriculum content for and with children. *Personal ecology is the individual child interrelating, interweaving, and interacting with the phenomena which make up her or his environment.*

The Distance-from-Self Criterion

I have combined the assumptions into a way of planning and selecting science content for children. The physical or cognitive distance from oneself is a criterion you can apply when you try to decide whether an activity is appropriate for the children you know. Figure 3 gives you a general idea of the distance-from-self criterion I mean. Here I am concerned with science learning, although I think the scheme could be applied much more widely to early childhood curricula building.

In Figure 3, the child's own self is central. The dimension radiating out in all directions represents development through time: the growth of the child's person and abilities, and the accumulation of experiences as learned. Around the periphery of this picture are examples of the adult sciences. How does a child grow from the center outward to encompass the learnings of the entire scheme? She or he goes through time and accumulates the experiences as he or she grows—if the experiences are there for the having.

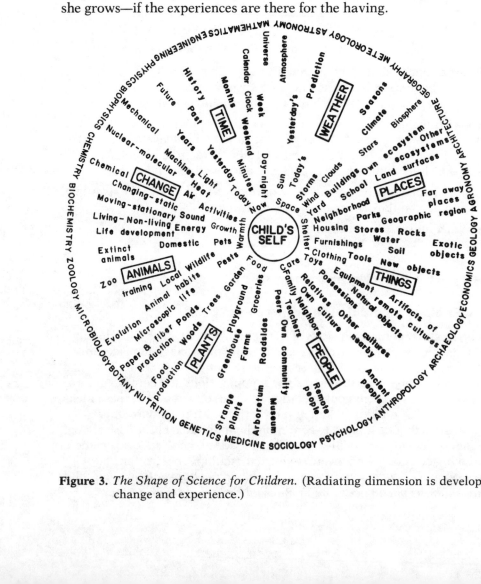

Figure 3. *The Shape of Science for Children.* (Radiating dimension is developmental change and experience.)

Most young children are still fairly close to the center, as the scope of their experiences is defined by Figure 3. I have divided significant science phenomena into eight groups: people, places, time, weather, objects or things, plants, animals, and change. The groups are arbitrary, however. You know well that all of these phenomena are interrelated and meshed, that friends and yards and running movements go together depending on the time of day and weather.

Each Picture Is Unique

I have tried to make a composite of examples in Figure 3. Each child would actually be an individual picture, and specific happenings in this individual life would replace the general phrases. Let's take some of Lennie's experiences in the weather and time groups as an example. Two-year-old Lennie experiences time through his stomach, in relation to his needs and the habits he has learned about food. He knows when it is time to eat; he has learned to see, hear, and smell the signs. He starts to stay in the kitchen underfoot at meal preparation time. He has begun to predict the sequence of a day through eating culturally characteristic food at given times. He also knows time through his clothing. Having his shoes taken off means naptime for Lennie, but being dressed in his pajamas means bedtime (night-into-morning).

Lennie does not know yet that the weather and temperature in his home city, New York, is cooler at night, that central heat is turned down to save fuel, or that his own body processes are slower when he is resting, but he does know he usually needs to be covered up with a blanket. That is important. He learns nighttime through his blanket. As he grows, he will learn today is now, that today's weather is cold and rainy, that night comes everyday after supper. Much later, he will learn there is a tomorrow, that tomorrow can be warm and sunny, that day and night roll around continually in a predictable diurnal cycle. He begins to learn some days are different than most, especially weekends and holidays. These days have different schedules. Then he will learn about days of the week having different names, and needing an account kept so one can tell which day it is. He will learn that the days have different names in a cycle of seven, a week, although nights do not have names.

He will also learn eventually about years and months, maybe in that order, because although months are shorter, they are also arbitrary. But a year makes sense in a climate where seasons change. As Lennie grows, he knows how old *he* is. An annual event—most likely his birthday, if celebrated—will probably be his first real experience-memory with a year of time. (And because Lennie is a highly valued person both at home and at school, his birthday enhances his self-esteem with his own special annual celebration.) He learns that growth, age, and time are related significantly for humans. Although Lennie learns hope for tomorrow, future time concepts generally come later, since Lennie can experience yesterday by remembering his own real activities. He will only have a vague speculation, then a guess, and at most a sophisticated prediction, about tomorrow. The future is a more difficult and inexact time concept than the past all through his life by the self-distance criterion.

As Lennie grows and develops further, he begins to relate time more widely and see how it interweaves with concepts of distance, for example, and movement. If his mother interrupts his television watching to send him to the store, he can run fast and miss very little of the program. If he walks along watching the sidewalk cracks and puddles, the trip to the store can take most of the afternoon. He is very unsure about measurements altogether, but measures of speed hold special fascination for his society, and by the time he is nine, he shows proper respect for a low time "zero to sixty" acceleration of vehicle speed, even though his family does not own an automobile.

Meanwhile, through his own time, Lennie is also experiencing the weather. He knows cold, warm, and hot air, and high or low humidity, both indoors and outside, by his own comforts, or mostly discomforts, which seem more significant. He also knows playing on the steps in the summer rain is in disfavor, though it feels good. He learns of many human activities which take place in relation to the weather: eating and drinking hot or cold food, or more or less food; eventually seasonal food comes to Lennie's attention. He experiences clothing changes, additions or subtractions, with the weather. Weather change can be vivid; storms are scary. Lennie learns about that very early in life.

Much later, Lennie learns about weather prediction. He watches and checks the weather person on TV—that person is not always right, either. He starts to think about signs of weather change, clouds and wind, for example. He does some predicting of his own. He puts a jar out on the roof and measures the rainwater which collects in it. He learns that he lives in a climate with a range of temperatures and weather types. He begins to find out that other people in other places live differently; when it is warm and sunny in New York, it may be raining on his cousins in North Carolina. When it is breakfast time for him, his aunt and family in Los Angeles are still sleeping in the dark—and his cousins in California have never seen snow.

The pasting of a sun or an umbrella on a boxed-off sheet of paper called a calendar is an indifferent activity for Lennie in kindergarten, although he likes to paste and enjoys matching the symbol with the weather he encountered on the way to school. A more meaningful record-keeping would be to put the symbols all along in a progressive row—with a moon or a bed or a blanket symbol in between. Then Lennie sees in an abstract way that day follows night follows day, which matches his experience. Lennie can begin to see the week cycle as he notes that weekends are different. He could choose his own symbol of weekend activities: He might suggest a baseball. Time, weather, and activities of humans all begin to coordinate into a learning and recording of sequences which still take a long time to grow into an understanding of the calendar.

The seasons are progressing, not within the framework of the months, or the calendar, but in a little child's experience. Understanding seasonal change means accounting for time, weather, and earth movements—too much for young children. For Lennie, the first day of spring is when he can go outside to play without his heavy jacket. Spring is not related to the calendar at all in his life, but he will learn at an early age to look forward to it. Lennie will be a long time understanding seasonal cycle, even though he lives in a climate where winter and summer are very different and the transitions of autumn and spring are notable. Wherever children live, the extraordinary significance of seasonal cycles of a year for all forms of life is a huge scientific understanding.

Concepts of time, weather, seasonal cycle, and climate are farther out on the self-distance criterion of some children than others:

> Marcella Running Deer lives near the northern shores of the big lake. Because she is learning her Chippewa science well, she knows winter means ice on the lake is thicker than a large tree, with the fish, cold and firm, swimming underneath. She will watch them be caught through a hole in the ice. She knows winter seasons-within-seasons, depending on the wind, the clarity of the air, the amount and quality of the snow. The snow crust will bear her weight, or it won't. It will show clear tracks, or it won't. It will stick to her feet, or it won't. She is beginning to understand the significance of each of these conditions. She fears the blowing blizzard. She learns why the sticky snow brings excitement. It can mean spring—a life-saving event each year at this time.

> Chester Jackson lives in a house on the outskirts of Casper, Wyoming. The seasons change, all right. Chester knows bitter winter cold and summers with sunny, hot, dry days and chilly nights. Spring comes abruptly; the older folks say you have one day to plant a garden before your lettuce dries up, but they laugh and wink, so he is not sure. He knows the wind brings all weather, so it probably brings spring. He already has the habit of scanning the western sky, like his daddy does, to take stock of the clouds. He still thinks the wind brings night, too. It brings everything else. Well, he now knows it does not bring the oil riggers and ranch hands into town on Saturday night, or does it?

> Taeko Kaawa spends her Hilo, Hawaii, winter wearing the same clothes she grew into a few months ago. There is occasional hard rain, as usual. Her father and his brother talk a great deal about football. But holidays and fluxes of tourists at the hotel where her mother works tell her more about the season than the weather. Since she knows little of seasonal temperature changes, she learns seasons by the school year—winter is when she goes to school; summer is when she stays home or with her grandparents on the farm. She can be of help in the summer on the farm because that is the peak of the vanda orchid harvest. Once on a holiday, her parents took her to see snow in the cones of Mauna Kea. But spring is a concept, not a happening, for Taeko.

All four of these children, Lennie, Marcella, Chester, and Taeko, are now eight-year-olds. All were recently taught in their third-grade classrooms that the first day of spring was March 20. But each person brought to that science lesson a unique background. And, regardless of previous experiences with spring seasonal changes, none of them is ready yet to understand the vernal equinox.

Nature Is Basic

Nature study has been given priority in early childhood science with good reason. It works. Children are fascinated by natural phenomena. It is their group, remember? They are natural phenomena. Understanding technology requires a young child to understand the products of an adult mind. That can be developmentally incompatible. I propose for your consideration a subcategory of the distance-from-self criterion which is the distance-from-nature criterion. It is easier and more appropriate for a child to trace the origin and development of a dandelion than a kitchen timer.

Children's questions often concern origins, whether natural or technological. Children are also interested in movement, change, and life itself, although their distinctions between living and not living may still need years of maturing. Children are interested in other people, other small or young creatures, other growth and the growth of others. All of these are nature interests.

Children's experience with nature is partly an access problem. Young children need protection and supervision; confinement to a small indoor space may be the usual solution. In major cities, access to large natural areas may cost money; therefore economics may influence the availability of nature experiences. Geography of a home region determines the limits of many children's experiences. Some children will not know what a beach is; others have not run or sledded down, felt or seen, the dip or swell of land into valleys and hills; still others have not experienced standing along the street and watching the rain collect and flow in the gutters.

Climate of a home region will determine the scope of weather, season, and many related sources of experience. Whether a child's home area is rural or urban makes a great deal of difference in his or her science life. A rural child may be ready to skim the cream from unhomogenized milk and churn butter. An urban child needs to trace the milk to its original source. Making butter, which many children do not eat at home, from purchased cream, which many children do not use or understand, is a far-removed exercise for a child who has never seen a cow. The teacher of urban young children has a special challenge to provide *natural experiences* and should have a special budget for it.

Physical sciences can come from basic natural experiences as soundly as biological sciences can. We have given examples of some of these phenomena earlier, bodies in motion and food preparation, for example. Physical science experiences likely to be naturally encountered seem more appropriate for very young children than hooking wires to a dry cell battery and understanding the sequence which causes a bulb to light. Children around four years old like a good show, especially a magic show. Many of the spectacular effects of adult-oriented science, such as "growing" chemical crystals into a "crystal garden" or working a magnet under a sheet of paper to cause iron filings to stand up on end, may be magic shows to young children. You will have to decide; ask yourself, "Is it likely to make *sense* to children?" Adults should be sensitive to young children's inability sometimes to distinguish between "magic" and science.

Applying the Distance-from-Self Criterion

How can science content make sense to young children? Ask yourself: What can I put into scientific focus that is part of a child's life today? What would be a significant happening to a child: A thunderstorm? A bulldozer? A cactus blossom? What are the science aspects of today's schedule at our center: The snack menu? The field trip? The play activity? What is this child ready to do on this day: In terms of interests? In terms of needs? In developmental readiness? In other settings? With other people? What can I add to this setting to supplement and enrich its "natural" offerings? Does my science curriculum build on what the child already knows? Does it relate to yesterday's activities? Does it also add something new? Is it likely to give a true (or correct or real) impression to children?

Look at Figure 3 again. *Think close to the center in beginning your science education program with young children.* Find out what they know, care about, and need. Let their interests, discussion, and questions indicate how natural, strong, and varied their everyday experiences are. Then you can add nature, strength, and variety as you deem they are needed. These are the content of your science. Think about the one-thing-at-a-time sequences which form an understanding for a young child. When in doubt, start with the child's part of a sequence or cycle. Begin where the child begins. Ecological thinking helps us understand the circularity and interdependence of all phenomena. Sometimes we break into a cycle of natural events artificially in order to study it. Make that break where the child enters the picture, where it affects the child, where the child can participate, feel, and sense. *Personal ecology can be the most basic science of all.*

YOUNG CHILDREN AND THE ENVIRONMENT

Young children can learn a sensible personal ecology from the beginning. Most of us grew to adulthood in a world we thought held endless resources. We developed in a culture which taught us resources were here for the purpose of serving human comfort. The only problem was to get our share. We learned that big is "good," bigger is "better," and "progress" means increasing size, speed, population, number of possessions, vividness, comfort, leisure, and ease. Now we have to reverse all that. We must think and live conservation of resources and careful limited use. We have to redefine progress as finding an effective survival technology. We must find ways to curtail size, reduce speed, limit population and possessions. We have to change our definitions of vividness, comfort, leisure, and ease. Giving up the balm of constant temperature control or giving in to a lowered speed limit is hard. We liked it another way. It is difficult to change, especially when we see change as curtailment of liberties, rights, or pleasures.

If we can reorient ourselves, we will not raise and educate children by false goals. We will not encourage them to aspire to an adult life-style they cannot have and the earth cannot support. Today's young children can grow responsibly into caretaking for the earth and its resources as a comfortable way of life. They can develop a life-style which is compatible with nature, which conserves the resources of the environment, and which provides satisfactions not defined by large size or number.

Early childhood education has a fine environmental tradition. Because it is based on the science of human-child development, including the biology of development, our educational heritage has respected the natural, organic being and biological function of each child. We have always been intensely aware of the child's personal environment as the setting for learning. More recently we have centered on child-environment interactions and the dynamics which surround and come from this ongoing exchange. We have emphasized these interactions as learning processes.

Some additions need to be made to the traditions of early childhood education science planning. Some new content, experiences, and the developments of new strengths are in order. We should emphasize the environment, and the role humans play in consuming the earth's riches. Humans affect their environments, and vice versa. The following are suggestions for focusing children and refocusing ourselves.

Life Skills: The First Step Toward a Better World Is Survival

Very young human children would not survive long unless adults or much older children cared for them. It is the nature of humans to need a long time to develop and mature. Even with young children, however, we have educational goals which are survival-oriented. We want children to "cope well" or "take care of themselves" or to "become independent." Learning to tie one's shoes is a survival skill; so are all the other early childhood independence-training and "school readiness" skills that are encouraged. Let's look at a few life skills young children begin to acquire. I have highlighted some which are environmental in purpose and scientific in experiential content.

Learning about Individuality.   Children can begin to learn about themselves and about personal attributes. Start with a full-length mirror. A mirror and mirror images are complex scientific experiences. Children can learn about their body parts and characteristics. A large mirror is useful so children can see their bodies in motion. They can begin to put together the inner feel and the outer look of body motion—movement in space. (Rockets to the moon are based on it.) Add objects for mirror study. Alicia doing a dance, Alicia holding a kickball, Alicia pouring water from a pitcher in one hand into a glass in the other hand—these are three distinctly different mirror experiences.

Teeth are especially significant as growth indicators for five- and six-year-olds. How about some science with teeth? What do teeth do? Why are they not all shaped alike? Help children think about what goes on in their chewing and manipulating mouthfuls of food of different kinds. How do our teeth compare to the teeth of other creatures? What do other species do with teeth?

And bones? Chicken bones can be carefully examined. They are harder in some parts of the body than others; along the breast bone on a chicken can be found a cartilaginous extension. Joints and their workings are fascinating, too—knees, elbows, fingers, toes. Do they all work alike? Are they like a chicken's wing or thigh-leg joints? What can humans do and not do with their joints? Can children feel their bones and joints? This suggests activities in movement and dance, with the additional focus on children's learning what is going on inside their bodies. To many young children, movement means life.

Hair and fingernails are important to very young children. These parts of the body grow noticeably fast, and are the objects of frequent grooming attention from nurturing adults. Hair and nails are fun to see magnified and to compare to samples from other people and from other forms of life. Using a pick or comb makes sense when children see a hair tangle magnified through a lens. Examine the magnified collection from under a fingernail. Look at the skin and skin lines around a fingernail. What do fingernails do? Besides scratch? Try to pick up a dried pea or a carrot seed.

Considering nails leads children to think about their fingertips. Nails protect these most sensitive and important areas. Why are fingertips special? Children can close their eyes and concentrate on fingertip sensations, surely some of the most delicate in all nature.

Fingers, too, call for special investigations. What are categorically called "small muscle activities" are really a whole series of magnificent body acts and sensations. Stop and think about some of these. Encourage children to pick up a cup by the handle, for instance, using one finger at a time. Are the fingers different from one another in strength and in the ease with which they work? Do the hands differ from one another in strength and skill? When children are doing crafts, eating, and other things with their hands and fingers, you have countless opportunities to focus them on these very special and very human body parts. Some good children's books are *Straight Hair, Curly Hair*, by Augusta Goldin; *Bodies*, by Barbara Brenner; and for help or for older children *The Story of Your Skin*, by Edith Lucie Weart.

Children can begin to learn about themselves and about personal attributes.

Individuality *is* scientific. Making finger, hand, and footprints with water or paint, or even bite impressions with teeth in soft wax or an orange peel, can be a way children begin to understand their own and others' individuality. Not only individual body shapes, colors, and textures, but individual feelings, preferences, and skills contribute to uniqueness. Grooming, self-care, and expressive activities have basic, natural, and scientific value and reasons.

As a child learns of herself or himself, she or he learns of origins and begins to think of destinies. Young children acquire much knowledge of life and development very early. It may take a lifetime to understand it. As children learn of infancy and growth, they can learn of advanced age, of growth slowing but never quite stopping, of changes and processes in development of many forms of life, both plant and animal.

Survival Techniques. Children can begin to learn how to procure, endeavor, and do in order to meet their own growth needs. What does life need? What are the conditions for growth? Children learn how and where to get drinks of water when thirsty and how and where not to. Help them learn to drink more and more often in hot weather and in dry climates, seasons, or schoolrooms. Help them learn that they take in fluids in many ways: drinking water, milk, juices; eating watery foods such as celery, lettuce, oranges, melons, juice-cicles; sucking ice cubes. Help them learn their bodies lose fluids in several ways; urination and perspiration are the most usual. Wetting the skin cools the body. It doesn't add fluid inside, but it's fun.

> *Children's Chatter: "Summer makes you 'spire. (A moment's pause.) No, that's not right. The sun makes you 'spire." (Pitts 1971b, p. 13)*

Children begin to be able to select food which supports growth, although reasons such as "it's good for you" do not hold much appeal. Adults have an uphill battle against the sugar-sellers for the minds and tastes of children. Children can learn good nutrition as a survival technique in life, rather than an adult-imposed system. Start with their experiencing a great variety of food, all of it nutritious. Feature nutritious food which is most familiar in their families and cultures—closest to the center, the child's own self. Children begin to learn what is edible and how it is made tasty or safe for eating. *Next to children's own bodies, food and fluid are probably the most important science experiences.* Food learning should take place everyday in a young child's life; food curriculum should be written into a *daily* schedule (Ferreira 1973; McIntyre 1975c).

Children begin to learn how to regulate themselves and their body rhythms. They learn to go to the toilet before they go to the playground. They begin to insert some thinking and some controls into processes of resting, going to sleep, wakening, and activating their bodies. They think about and experiment with breathing. What causes fast, heavy breathing? How do sleeping people breathe? They begin to learn there are many ways of regulating temperature so the body is comfortable. They learn about using clothing and other body coverings according to temperature perception. They begin to notice and judge environmental temperature conditions. Is it "hot" or "cold" outdoors? Would being wet all over make you comfortable and cool or shivery?

Think how many specific science experiences you do with children which contribute to their learning to take care of themselves. This is some of the most important work you do. Directing your own attention to the science aspects of this teaching may help you to emphasize it with children. Think through and discuss the following example as a survival lesson (or two or three) for primary school children.

> Kim Lu liked the feel of the cotton boll. She rubbed it on her cheek, looked at it carefully, tried to imagine how it looked on the plant in the farmer's field, like the one in her teacher's picture. She felt the soft pieces of fabric, some were like a dress, some like her ribbed corduroy pants, some like underwear, some like blue jeans, different from one another but all made of cotton from cotton bolls like the one she had in her hand.

> On the days that followed, the children looked at raw wool, yarn, and woolen fabrics. They saw pictures of sheep grazing, being sheared, and being fed in the winter snow. They saw pictures of spinning wheels and spinning. They saw pictures of looms. One day a woman with beautiful, quick hands came to visit. She demonstrated knitting and weaving on a small loom. The children took turns using the loom. The next day they wove paper strips into mats.

> On still other days, they saw synthetic fabrics—nylon, polyester knits, and woven materials, and acrylic or orlon yarns and fabrics. Some felt like the woolens and the cotton fabrics, too. They saw pictures of oil wells and coal mines. There were some pictures of big machines in factories where these fibers were made instead of being grown. Machines pushed the yarns out of very small holes like pressed cookies or riced potatoes. Kim Lu found it hard to believe these fibers came from coal and petroleum just like the gasoline in the car.

> Kim Lu liked the days when they lined a sieve with a fabric sample and poured water through. The water went through some fabrics very fast. Other fabrics seemed to hold the water, at least a little while. And with some pieces, she could watch the water spread out into the fabric. Teacher said this was "absorbing." Water seemed to cool most of the material, too. Now it was easy to remember what it felt like to get caught in the rain. But the wool stayed warm-feeling, and did not seem very wet, even when she could squeeze water out. It was like a sponge. No wonder sheep could stay out in the snow and rain.

> Days later, the children also examined some used and very worn pieces of garments they had each brought from home to school for rags. Each child had his or her own personal mop-rag. They used the rag pieces to wipe tables, clean up spills, and dry off the playground equipment after a shower. Some rags worked better, and felt better, than others. Kim Lu decided cotton was her favorite mop, especially the rag made out of her old "holey" summer shirt.

Learning about Other Forms of Life.   Children can begin to learn the life requirements of other animals and plants. All gardening, sprouting, seeding, and houseplant care activities are life skills. All pet care activities and learning and caring about the needs and habits of all other plants and animals, domestic and wild, are survival learnings. It is important that children are able to observe similarities and differences between their own needs and those of other life forms. We should also encourage children to attend to the links among us. All forms of life are interrelated. Different forms of life need and depend on one another. These relationships form an important part of science.

If you were to make a chart called "The Growth Conditions of Common Plants and Animals in My Area," could you fill it in? Wouldn't you want to know the following information about each entry?

What are its nourishment needs? What does it eat? Drink? How? How much? When?

Under natural conditions, where do its food and water come from? Can the conditions be copied?

How does it keep warm? Cool off? Does it have any characteristic temperature reactions? Does it shiver, curl up, puff out? Does it perspire, wilt, pant?

What is its sleep-wake pattern? Is it diurnal? Nocturnal? Seasonal? What is its need for sunshine?

How, where, and in what form does it eliminate? Do the (animal) feces have characteristic forms? Does elimination have other significance, for example, territory-marking?

Where does it live, most likely? Does it seek or make any kind of shelter? What kind? Under what conditions?

What are its reproductive patterns? Readiness or courtship signs? How does new life come to be? How does it grow?

What are the major developmental periods of its life? What is the usual length of its life cycle?

How does it protect itself and its way of life? How does it survive? What is the biggest threat to its life?

What are its physical characteristics at various developmental stages? Color? Size? Does it make sound? Various sounds? Under what conditions?

These are things children want to know, too. Try making a chart of such information for the forms of life the children are most likely to encounter, for example, squirrels, dogs, guppies, violets, and maple trees. See how many ways you can think of to help children experience the answers to these questions.

Environmental Learning. Children begin to be aware of many qualities in environmental phenomena. What clues tell them that a sparrow or a building is "old"? How do they tell "baby" plants? What are the color differences between alfalfa sprouts grown in a dark cupboard and alfalfa sprouts grown in a tray of soil in the window? Which part of the blackboard is wet and which is dry? How do they know? Can they see what happens when they blow on the wet part? The dry part? What does weathering do to wood? To asphalt? To concrete?

Qualities of age, stage of development, color, moistness, texture, and many, many other sensory distinctions provide information about the environment. Children can be helped to pay attention to the details they see and clues they use in making judgments. As they grow older, children will be able to consider more than one quality in determining such characteristics.

Relationship to All Forms of Life.   Children can learn to respect all forms of life. No life should be hurt, frightened, or needlessly destroyed. I have mentioned a child's feeling of closeness with pets. It should be expanded to other life, not ignored as "childish" or sentimentalized by "Isn't that cute?" Since all forms of life are affiliated in the biological scheme, we are supporting a scientific point of view. This means we care for pets and gardens, but leave wildlife and wild plants alone. It means the release of insects or tadpoles that have been detained in a jar for closer observation. It means children participate in letting them go. If pests are to be eliminated, flies swatted, or cockroaches stomped, children should understand the threat and the reason in order to see this as the exception to the rule. Pests are creatures out of place and out of control by human definition. The pest threat becomes greater as human population increases, because garbage and sewage increase. As we support our own lives, we also support ever-increasing numbers of pests. But if we find a ladybug (an insect which is a natural pest-controller) indoors, we should make a group project out of returning it to a carefully selected bush in the yard.

Properties of Substances.   Children begin to acquire all of the years of experience which will eventually help them to distinguish between what is alive, what has been alive but is not now, and what never had life. They begin to learn some important distinctions between natural and person-made things. Such understandings do not arrive suddenly or in a vacuum. Though some children have real confusions, young children mostly need time and experience to explore these qualities of life, movement, change, and to learn the properties of substances.

Using Natural Resources.   Experiences with water, sand, soil, mud, clay, rocks, air, sticks, leaves, wind, and sounds are basic environmental studies. Play activities and explorations with natural materials of all kinds cannot be overemphasized. Creative activities with *natural materials* should take the place of at least half of those you plan with the traditional purchased media (paints, paste, fingerpaint, paper, etc.) and could replace these materials much more often. Pictures can be drawn in sand. Many of us live near places where clay can be dug or mud can be made. All of us can get to water.

Have you ever tried coloring and dye-making with natural materials? Nutshells, dried flowers, and common waste items like onion peels make beautiful coloring. Try the toys of the earth: sticks and stones, raindrops, and breezes. Play activities with water and sand, understanding air and wind, experimenting with sound—these are the beginnings of environmental awareness. Here is where the understanding of pollution and misuse must originate. Here is where we start to learn the conservation of the earth's riches—when we learn to value them, feel close to them, and good about them.

Exploring the Environment.   As children learn of properties and characteristics, they also begin to understand mixing and compounding. What mixes and what does not? What is it made of? The ingredients that go into bread, for

As children learn of properties and characteristics, they also begin to understand mixing and compounding. What mixes and what does not? What is it made of?

example, are complex and fascinating. Each has its own identity. None by itself is bread. Bread depends on the right combination and treatment. Each ingredient makes its contribution; different combinations of similar ingredients make different breads. (That yeast is alive and brings qualities of life to bread may be too hard to understand.) Think about the ingredients of other common substances.

Careful observation by children—attention, taking apart, and experimenting—is part of the analysis processes which answer "What's it made of?" What kinds of mixtures can be taken apart and what kinds cannot? Examining a milk carton can mean scraping the wax, feeling it, and exposing the heavy paper layer underneath. It can lead to trying out the water retention of waxed and unwaxed paper or of milk cartons which have been scraped. It might lead to other wax inquiry. Bring in a honeycomb. Help children shine shoes; do a batik; make a candle; seal a note with a wax blob; watch camellia leaves in the rain; water or mist a jade plant; fix a leaky paper cup with some paraffin; watch water roll from a duck's back; make muffins, placing milk and oil together. Wax or oil or many oily or fatty substances do not mix with water. That is useful knowledge. How do you blend them to make mixing happen? How do you separate them to prevent mixing from happening?

Making Environmental Elements Meaningful.   Children begin to be aware of the components of different environments. They can compare and contrast indoors and outdoors. How can they tell? Attending to differing sounds and combinations of sounds, smells, and key visual and temperature clues can help children distinguish environments. What does wind tell us? Feelings of dryness or moisture? Children can compare home and school, neighborhood and downtown, city and country, busy street and park. What elements of each of these places are meaningful to children? Ask them. How do the elements an individual child attends to fit together to create a feeling of the place itself? Where are the components of a given environment located in relation to one another? Trees do not grow under rocks; buildings are not built in the middle of streets—it works better that way. Children can benefit if they stop and give it some attention.

Basic Learnings.   As children learn of themselves and the environment, they learn of health and hazards. Have you thought of some good additions to the list of precautions in Chapter Three? As children learn of their own bodies, they also become aware of health needs and dangerous conditions for themselves, other persons, and other forms of life.

Topography and directional studies or orientation to a neighborhood are great unknowns. Children do learn their way around an area. Landmarks, directional sense, movement in space and remembering it, feelings of sidedness or laterality within the body must all contribute. Young children can be helped to focus on environmental clues. In rural areas, children learn east from west by noticing things like the direction of light on a hillside and its shadow, sunsets, prevailing winds, and cloud movements. Children who grow up around adults who must survive on the land learn these phenomena very early. City children notice unique neighborhood buildings and features: the color of a door, the shape of a special window, a tile roof, a weeping willow tree.

> Elton was a competent, five-year-old Head Starter. His mother had walked him to the school center all last year, teaching him carefully about crossing streets. Now, with the new baby at home, she usually expected Elton to walk the quiet block-and-a-half in the neighborhood by himself. It was several weeks before the teacher discovered that Elton was actually walking three-and-a-half blocks each day, going carefully around the middle block in his route to avoid a large threatening dog. He was able to relate a number of his landmarks: "the bush with prickles," "the slivery fence," and the "sand pile"—a run-off from a vacant lot. He knew each in sequence, depending on whether he was coming or going.

Importance of Maintenance.   Children can begin to learn to respect and revere maintenance activities for inanimate objects. Young children often reflect in dramatic play the importance of these activities to adults and their appeal to children. They "oil" the tricycle with sand or water. Why not oil? Activities we do to protect or prolong the use of things usually have a scientific basis. Lubricating, drying, watering, and other maintenance are of great interest to children. They can help, and begin to understand why we put wagons in the shed, keep the garden tools indoors to prevent rust or theft, close the sandbox to keep cats out, put dishes in the cupboard to keep the dust off them, are careful not to break fragile items. All the environmental grooming and preservation activities we call "cleaning" are environmentally sound and purposeful activities. Children should share them. Maintaining the objects we have in good working order means we do not have to use new resources to replace them. Maintaining them clean and safe means protecting ourselves and others. Children can also learn from mistakes, theirs and ours. If a metal spinning top is left out in the rain, it may be damaged and not work. Taking it apart to find out why is an important environmental science experience.

Value of Repair.   Children begin to acquire crafts and skills which may later prove important. They can participate in making simple repairs. Pasting, gluing, taping, bonding, and sealing are ways of getting broken or torn edges together as well as being creative activities. Sewing and woodworking are important *repair* skills, too. Repairing means saving new resources that would otherwise be used in replacement goods.

Field trips to garages or shoe repair shops are sometimes overlooked. Ask a plumber or a person who fixes clocks or meters or suit pants to visit and bring some tools and maybe a project. Take the time to explain and show children how you are fixing an object. Help and applaud when children fix things. People who repair and fix should be society's heroes.

> *Children's Chatter: Jennie Lee, as she examined a wobbly trike, "I could mend this if I had some suppliers" (meaning pliers). (Pitts 1975c, p. 21)*

Creatively Using Materials on Hand.   Children learn to make gifts and items of useful and decorative beauty from materials at hand. Children know what to do with plastic packing wiggles and egg cartons. Help them appreciate themselves and others who beautify without buying. Share your own creations and their uses with children, too. (We are often afraid that we will be providing an example which children will copy, thereby suppressing their creativity. It's a wise caution. But it is also wise for an adult to be a person who does interesting things with materials, and for children to know it. Adults are models; children want to be like them. Adults can do adult things with materials. Children can make the distinction if you can.)

Children can begin to appreciate themselves for creative devising. Makeshifting and scrounging are teacher traditions worth passing on. Early childhood teachers eventually learn never to throw out anything safe until they see if children can find a use for it.

Emphasis on Variety of Attributes.   Let's alert ourselves to the ways we teach children to value largeness in size and number, and start to do it differently. When children are babies, a favorite game is "So-o-o Big," with the child stretching up on tiptoes. Early childhood centers have games, finger plays, and songs which are variations of this theme. Instead, how about "So-o-o Competent" or "So-o-o Verbal" or "So-o-o Able-to-Do" or "So-o-o Smart" or "So-o-o Understanding" or "So-o-o Loving"? All of these attributes have maturing components and are signals of growth, too. In the fall, we say to children we have not seen since spring, "My, how you've grown!" indicating their increase in height. Is physical growth really the most socially acceptable source of pride in oneself? Isn't that what we teach children? No wonder older children have some problems in self-acceptance when they figure out physical growth is not valued in adolescents and adults. No wonder obesity is a national disease.

We let our values of size and number come through in other ways, too. "What a *great, big* picture you are making—that's fine." Or, "Look at *how many* pictures you have made! Isn't that great." (Give that child a medal for paper consumption? If it is so great there has to be a better reason than sheer number.) Size and number are components of many phenomena. Size and number vary naturally. Some trees are very small; some are very large; most are in between. Insects and fish produce many eggs; birds produce few eggs; most reptiles are somewhere in between. These are number and dimension learnings. The cultural overlay of valuing massiveness or numerousness should be recognized and the attitude must change.

As child development persons, we value children's growth highly. We work for it. It is our goal. However, we need to be sure we do not generalize that all growth is progress or define improvements by increasing number or size. Of course a child's growing is good, exciting, and beautiful when it is biologically appropriate. It just does not deserve the social load we ask it to bear. The feeling "I am good because I grow" can carry a young child for a while, but it is limited later on, when growth slows down. What does a child do for the next trick? In science, we should work on recognition of many self-attributes, many aspects of growing. Let's equally emphasize variety and diversity in size and number and strengths in other attributes as well as physical growth. When children get older, they learn to count and account. Then many quantitative activities become possible: measuring, statistical prediction, mathematical recordkeeping, etc. This is where size and number belong.

Use of Color.   We have lore in early childhood education which has taught us that children prefer bright, saturated, primary colors. Do they? The literature on young children's color preferences is thin and inconclusive. Maybe young children like bright colors in all their goods for the same reason they "like" salty baby food—because it pleases the adults who buy it. We saturate young children with colors. Perhaps our own visual appetites for vividness have grown insatiable. It appears that way when we persist in coloring food artificially to make it more acceptable (or saleable)—even when the safety of those coloring agents is questionable. Is breakfast cereal really more appealing when it resembles a paint box? Did anyone ask you whether you like orange cheese? Do you know that no cheese in the world is naturally bright orange? Learning (or re-learning) to see beauty in the soft natural colors of the earth's materials may be a real challenge to adults. It appears, since artificial coloring materials and procedures continue to be implicated as health and environmental hazards, that we should take the challenge quickly and begin to withdraw ourselves and children from the "great color splurge."

Modern child development persons may be the only people in the world who think of "conservation" as phenomena occurring in the cognitive structuring of children's minds. Most people think of conservation activities as saving resources and preserving the balances of ecosystems. As I interpret it, these are not basically different concepts. Conserving means saving, holding, preserving, and protecting a condition, whether that condition is a species of animal or an idea in your head. It can mean leaving a condition unchanged or attending to changes that balance it. It can mean understanding an overall picture, idea, or system and how changes help to keep things the same and in what ways. Jean Piaget has drawn our attention to specific kinds of sensorimotor conservations (identity, memory, object permanence, perceptual constancies, etc.) and of operational conservations based on reversibility (conservations of number, quantity, volume, weight, etc.). Piaget (1971), psychologist and biologist, discusses analogies between biological conservations and human intelligence conservations. David Elkind concludes from Piaget's work:

> The essence of the theory can be simply stated: the child discovers conservation— permanence across apparent change—with the aid of reason. It is by reasoning about his experience that the child is able to overcome illusions and discover how things really are. . . . By abetting the child's discovery of conservations, we help him establish the intellectual security which is the necessary starting point for seeking out fresh encounters with the environment. The more the child becomes aware of the truth inherent in the saying "always changing, always the same," the more he will look upon new experience as a challenge to his intelligence rather than a threat to his existence. (1970, pp. 4-6)

Experiences with science and nature should be a challenge rather than a threat. Before they "discover conservation," children could be imposed upon by the very real threats to the world of resource misuse and imbalances in cycles. Fear without understanding may result. Young children are not ready for the full-blown environmental concepts of conservation and balances in ecosystems. A teacher who consumes time and resources trying to teach children something they are not ready to learn is in violation of good conservation practice.

Conservation of resources and of the earth's systems presumes the inclusion of human activities in all the balance (or imbalance) equations. These are very complicated ideas, even for adults. It is hard to understand something so vast, so awesome. It makes sense to assume children will *understand* more fully the need for replanting trees and preventing soil erosion when they know that pouring water from a short, fat container into a tall, thin one does not change the amount of water—only the container. It "saves" the water. However, children enjoy planting a fir tree or putting the soil back in a hole they have dug. These nature conservation activities are appropriate because they are enjoyable and productive activities. It seems logical that they are also good beginnings for later development of responsibility and stewardship of the earth. A hole is not only to dig, but to refill. So is a strip mine.

Look at a list of basic biological conservation practices: proper use of natural materials; consumption based on need, not desire; replacement and recycling; protection of resources; intelligent control of technology and production; preservation of rare and endangered plants, animals, and ecosystems; population control; preservation of diversity and variety in species and in cultures. Conservation means making sure the world is "always changing, always the same." Children can learn conservation practices as habits and as a reasonable way of life—not as a "cause." They can learn through their own bodies and in their own kitchens and backyards. Learning and understanding will take years and years of experience with materials and processes. You can provide some of them. You can help by being very aware. You can help by doing conservation activities yourself. You can help by knowing why you do them and being able and ready to discuss reasons.

Conservation of Paper

Use plastic dishes for all food service. They should be dishwasher-safe. It does not use as many resources to wash dishes as it does to use disposable service. Limit your use of paper cups, plates, etc. Virtually all paper comes from trees. We cannot grow them as fast as we are using them— we keep dipping into the reserves.

Keep a small terry cloth or cotton hand towel, hung by a tape loop, in the bathroom or washing and personal grooming area. Each child should have a hook labeled with his or her name and a symbol (preferably of the individual's own choice). Change the towels as needed, launder, and use for years and through several groups of children. Although laundering cloth is more work, it is better than using disposable paper.

Each child can have a plastic (dishwasher-safe) cup with his or her name and/or symbol on it. Fingernail polish works for lettering and lasts through a number of washings; it can be renewed as needed. The cup is kept within the child's reach and used exclusively for his or her own drinks of water. A water fountain that is readily accessible is even better.

Use single-wipe, small-size tissues for runny noses. You may have to obtain them through a hospital supplier.

Use rags and sponges for mopping-up activities.

Encourage children to use both sides of craft paper of any kind.

Help children experiment with and learn about paper as it is used. Note that wax or plastic coating aids water retention. What soaks through more easily, a paper napkin or a brown bag? Soak newsprint and examine it. Notice, when someone is doing chalk-on-wet-paper crafts, how easily the paper tears. Try fingerpainting on various papers. Tabletops also work well as a surface which can be washed and reused. So does a slab of plastic-coated wood or composition board. Dry paper that has been soaked and use it again. Help children gain a deep appreciation of paper—it is one of the items which may be increasingly rare and expensive within their lifetimes.

Encourage car pools and walking pools among the families and staff.

Turn on lights only when you need them.

Celebrate and use sunshine: to dry clothes and towels, to see fine details of a project, to grow green plants, to enjoy.

Place rocks in the sun for some time. When warm, they can be brought inside. Help children learn how rocks, metals, etc., hold heat for a period of time. They should learn about these substances in relation to the cold, too.

Use appliances only when necessary. Turn on a radio, record player, or tape-recorder only when children intend to listen attentively. Avoid using these devices to provide "background music."

Help children understand heating and cooling processes.

Help children understand energy-rest relations. What uses energy? What saves energy? Young children will be only beginning to understand. You can help them focus on rest and activity cycles.

Conservation of Other Materials

Use tape of all types sparingly. String is reusable; tape is not.

Use a metal dispenser with refill rolls if you need cellophane or other paper-plastic tape. Avoid buying tape on a plastic throwaway dispenser.

Avoid disposable ballpoint and felt-tip markers for children's use—and your own. More material is discarded than is used.

You and children are good at reusing plastic containers and bags. But do you avoid buying plastic in the first place? You should—it is not biodegradable and is difficult to recycle.

Conservation of Water

Revere and respect water. All living creatures and plants need it. Children will come to know its importance when adults begin to realize it. Children already know its delights—a good basis for reverence.

Encourage drinks from the faucet or fountain without running the water to "get it cold." If you and/or children prefer cold water, keep a jug in the refrigerator. This uses less energy and wastes no water.

Teach children to use a sink stopper or plug. They can learn to fill a basin of water for washing hands, cleaning, sponging, or playing in. None of these activities should be done under running water. Provide tubs, pails, and dishpans for water activities. Carry any uncontaminated and unsoapy, but slightly used, water to the garden if possible.

Teach children to flush only after use. Flushing a toilet is not a play activity. It may use as much as six gallons per flush.

Use a basin of water to wash vegetables, peel potatoes, etc., with children. Never do these activities under running tap water.

Conservation of Food

Food is for eating, but it is also for learning. Ferreira (1973) gives a good introduction and many activities for natural learning through natural food.

Children must learn to respect and value food from the beginning and without exception. This will mean some new thinking for some adults. Craft activities should not be done with edible substances which render the food inedible. This does not mean that food cannot be played with—it can; many activities can be done with the food as long as it stays clean and is eaten eventually. Careful examination of a pile of dried peas, or even running-the-fingers-through, can be a delightful experience—before the peas go into the soup. But respecting food does mean that early childhood centers and parents of preschoolers should avoid making play dough and paste with flour, salt, cornstarch, soda, or any other food combinations. That is going to be hard to change. Ceramic clays (earthenware, stoneware, etc.) have much more satisfactory qualities for the craft activities. If you maintain clay well, it will last for years—and is certainly cheaper than foodstuffs. Buy your paste. Use flour for a loaf of bread. Avoid using potatoes or carrots for printing activites; printing can be done with styrofoam wastes, rocks, concrete, or old linoleum. Weed pods and inedible grasses, stems, and seeds make great collage material—but rice, barley, corn, and dried beans should be cooked and eaten. Paint with water—save the milk for the lunch table. Eat the macaroni and cranberries, and use plastic wastes and dry weed pods for stringing and decorating.

Children do understand and share feelings of joy and satisfaction through gardening, harvesting, and eating their own food. Help them also to share garden produce.

Teach appreciation for great variety, and help children experience new foods, especially plant foods and sources of high vegetable protein—beans, peas, soybean products.

Save your food scraps for pets or compost.

Conservation of Soil

Think in terms of prudent land use. Children should learn about farming. Most food comes from the land. Urban children need special experiences planned for them.

Visit a construction site with children. Note levels of soil and their differences in the excavation. Sometimes children can see these soil levels in holes they dig. If possible, take samples from the levels. You might even try growing seeds in your samples. The topsoil in an area which has not been dug previously is the productive soil. As you watch a large bulldozer or mechanized shovel at work, you will note the topsoil is turned over and lost in many construction projects. New soil has to be brought from elsewhere for the landscaping. The world cannot afford such wasteful practice very long.

Begin to share with children a reverence for topsoil. Good soil, that which grows food and fiber well, is a distinctive resource, like wood and minerals. When topsoil is destroyed, buried, or eroded, it cannot be replaced within many human generations, if ever.

Examine kinds of soil: sand, humus, clay, gravel, loam mixtures. Children can see and feel the differences. Compare them in good light and magnification. Grow, or try to grow, seeds in different soils. Purchase potting soil for plants. How does it compare to samples of street dirt, playground grit, alleyway gravel, sandbox sand? "All dirt is not alike" should be a minimal outcome learned.

Food-growing should be an activity that takes first place where soil is good. People can build houses and sprawling suburbs on poor quality land; good land should be saved to feed them.

Filter the run-off water after a rain. See what makes it "muddy." It may be your garden soil going down the drain. Rivers and streams are interesting filtering and observing sites, too.

On a windy day, you and children can look at what is actually blowing around. It may be soil or pollutants—soot and other solid wastes. If a wind gust hits your sandpile, help children watch it. Watch a graveled alley or road on a windy day or after a car drives by. Look at what moves dirt around. What holds it in place? Plants! You do not see clouds of dust rising from the lawn, or the forest, or a midsummer bean field.

Leave a tabletop or some dark surface until it becomes very dusty. You and children can then examine some of the dust; use a magnifier. What is it? Where do you suppose it comes from?

Examine, with children, the filters of your furnace, air conditioner, or other air-filtering system. See what is filtered from the air.

Changes, Chains, and Sequences

All science action is change. Changes are interesting and lively. Children seem to like changes, as long as they are not too much or too disruptive. Sequences are series of changes which depend on or relate to one another. Cycles are circular, spiral, or spherical sequences, either in fact or in their interconnections. Natural cycles are usually self-perpetuating.

I have discussed the different emphases environmental education requires: learning about movements, changes, transitions, relationships, and linkages between phenomena. This is where the action is. Children begin to put together systems of anticipation and expectations of changes (Isaacs 1974). This adds excitement. Children learn about growth and development. These are changes very close to themselves. They learn about metamorphoses, the abrupt form changes in the development of some creatures such as frogs and butterflies. Perhaps because they are abrupt, dramatic, or surprising, these changes are especially fascinating. Children learn about chemical and physical processes and changes, such as dissolving, solidifying, condensing, floating, sinking, etc. Combining ingredients may change them. Mixing flour into the cookie dough changes the flour and the dough; neither will be the same again. But mixing raisins into the dough does not work the same way. You can still pick out the raisins and have the dough plain. Children are pleased to discover color changes when mixing paints or the texture changes found through kneading bread. Fat congeals, chicken broth gels, ice cubes melt. Things can be made into other things, or they can be treated, or changed. Whenever you are doing something like this with children, some science is involved. *Highlight it.*

Cause-and-effect is the kind of relationship we think of when someone says "science." These are not the only kinds of change sequences, but they are important ones. Knowing the cause is going a long way toward solving a problem. As children grow older, they become more interested in these relations.

If you track things back far enough in origin, you will find natural resources being used, since all things in the world are made of natural resources. But these long sequences in retrospect are not right for young children. If they can see the cow being milked, they know. If they can shell and grind the peanuts into peanut butter, they know. If they can plant, harvest, and eat carrots, they know. Some sequences are easier to understand than others. You do not have to teach a whole sequence. One link at a time still builds a sequence eventually in a child's experience.

Some natural changes and sequences can be observed over a few minutes, a few hours, or a day. These shorter ones children will follow with great energy.

101
YOUNG
CHILDREN
AND THE
ENVIRONMENT:
CHANGES

Here are a few other ideas to help you think about changes, chains, and sequences.

Plan for the time required. Some natural changes and sequences can be observed over a few minutes, a few hours, or a day. These shorter ones children will follow with great energy. Think about: the weather in a storm, an icicle melting, shadows of persons, tulips blooming, mice having babies, robins making a nest, wetting smooth rocks to observe patterns, water running off and away after a rain, a wet sidewalk drying in the sun, a pinwheel in the wind, a balloon being blown up or deflated. Some changes and sequences take longer and require repeated observations and some attention to long-term comparison activities: autumn leaves turning color, young guppies growing, a sweet potato sending out vines and roots in water, trees budding and leafing, beans sprouting, an old iron skillet rusting, mold growing on a lemon rind kept in a warm dark place, dandelions budding-blooming-going-to-seed-and-blowing-away. Here is where your support, your own excitement, your own sustained interest, will help children continue with the experience, or come back to it.

Help children learn where food comes from and what it is made of. Food chains are among the most important sequences we know. Pavoni et al. define a food chain as "the transfer of food energy from plants, through a series of consumers, each being eaten by another" (1974, p. 53). All food originates in plants, which make the food from sunshine, water, and nutrients in the soil. The hamburger at lunch went through an extra consumer besides the plants (unless it was made of soybeans); the food chain was longer than the food chain for the celery sticks. Generally, the longer the food chain before it reaches the human, the more energy it takes to produce the food (or the "less efficient" it is). This is not something young children will understand—but you should know about it. Children do learn the basic components: All of our food comes from somewhere; all can be traced back to plants; plants need water, light, and soil; cows and sheep eat grass and grain; pigs, chickens, turkeys also eat grain; fish eat water plants and small animal life in water (or fish food which is a substitute made from a mixture of grains and animal products); humans do not generally eat animals which eat other animals; plants produce great food variety and we increase the variety by processing.

Do a lot of cooking with children. All of our food selection, preservation, preparation, and cooking activities are based on our knowledge of changes and sequences affecting foodstuffs. Either we want to bring about change, or we want to prevent it, in our food. We chew food in order to change it. We wash food in order to prevent change in it—or in us! There are many good sourcebooks giving suggestions for food activities with young children, for example, Austin Association for the Education of Young Children 1973, Carmichael 1969, McIntyre 1975c, Ferreira 1973. If the children are older, and you are ready for intense science with food, see *Science Experiments You Can Eat* (Cobb 1972).

Go back and read again about life skills in the preceding sections. Every one of these requires an understanding of changes and relationships. Pull out some of these processes and list them, if only to give yourself a new point of view on some old ideas. Start with breathing, seeing, hearing, feeling, tasting, smelling, and sensing in every way.

103
YOUNG
CHILDREN
AND THE
ENVIRONMENT:
CHANGES

Children can begin to learn the relation of energy to work and the need for rest. They are related. Many preschoolers have already learned that food and/or rest and/or air intake have some relation to their ability to play vigorously. Mostly they have been told, or have overheard remarks like "What did you eat for breakfast this morning?" or "Maybe if I got all that sleep, I could run fast too." Children associate heavy, fast breathing with running and jumping. If they compare one another's panting, one another's pulse, or one another's heartbeat (use a stethoscope if possible) before and after jumping, they can begin to know that parts of their bodies besides their feet and legs are involved. Another link is added to the sequence they will eventually understand.

Children may have learned that physical exercise makes them hungry. Many of them seem to know that food helps them move. TV advertisers make sure they learn that lesson early. So, what makes a fish go? A tractor? A radiator? Observations of themselves, adults, and other animals can contribute to the beginning of understanding of energy and activity-rest cycles in animals, humans, and plants. These cycles are very significant to well-being and productivity. These experiences may even make more sense to children in scheduling their own rest than adult-enforced group rest periods or naps. What do people find restful? Exciting? What things happen that make people move fast? Children have many observations which are pertinent. Help them listen to different kinds of music. What do they feel like doing—resting, or moving around?

Think about mechanical, electrical, and solar energy. What work do they do? What makes a tricycle go? A flashlight? A toothbrush? How does a saw work? Why does the wood get warm? Feel the windowsill in the shadow, then feel the one across the room in the sun. What are the differences in them? What are the differences in a few drops of water placed in two plastic lids, one on each windowsill? Cover a small plant with a drinking glass and observe what happens. With older children, place a full jar of water on a sunny windowsill. Mark the waterline each day with a wax pencil, or do this with two similar jars, only cover one tightly. Do a variation in a graduated cylinder so older children can measure the water loss or replace the water loss at the end of the week, measuring the replacement water with an eyedropper, etc.

Children can begin to learn about healing and fixing—one link at a time. Finding out why someone is sick or why a top will not work are significant environmental problem-solving activities. "What's wrong?" is a human question to be pursued with diligent attention. Often, in these unraveling processes, we track sequences. The sequence of behavior we call "diagnosis" or "troubleshooting" is also known as scientific method.

The concepts of circular sequences and spherical systems are complex even for adults. But these ideas are basic to us and science. Friedrich Froebel thought the child's first toy object, or "gift" in a carefully graded sequence of experiences, should be a ball. Balls, hoops, loops, wheels, tops—these all give tangible go-around experiences. For more sophisticated children, you could introduce sequential stories, both continuous and discontinuous. A good source is *Arm-in-Arm* by Remy Charlip (1969).

Am I suggesting the child learns to conserve the world's resources by turning a trike upside down and spinning a wheel? Yes, it is a good analogy. This kind of experience may be fundamental to a later understanding. The earth is essentially a closed system of materials, and life on earth will last only as long as everything stays in circulation, in balance, and in sequence. An imbalanced cycle, a population grown too large for its food or water supply, too much of the wrong kind of garbage for time and decomposers to handle—these are like a flat tire or a wobbly wheel. They will not work very well or for very long.

Most of the recycling the children learn will be from your own activities (Crase and Jones 1974). Since young children are generally one-thing-at-a-time people, the sequences and relationships of recycling may be too complex for full understanding. But they can begin. Everything relates; maybe you can provide one link. That's a start. You can certainly be aware of the potential power of your example—we learn so much before we remember how or when. Recycle everything you can. Be sure children share these activities and your reasons for doing them. Here are a few activities children can share:

Do you recycle trash? Trash sorting is a good exercise in classification of materials for young children. What are the trash rules in your area? Why? Some cities recycle glass, metals, and reusable paper. A few cities even burn trash which cannot be economically recycled and use the energy from this process as a power source. If you are not so fortunate, maybe you can locate a recycling depot which will at least take bundled newspaper or flattened aluminum cans. Be sure any old aluminum utensils or "disposable" frozen food containers are recycled. Make sure children know that any recycled item will be used for some purpose, and that reuse is worth the work you must do to recycle the material. If you have no outlet for recycled trash in your location, help children do this sorting activity occasionally if only for ease of handling the trash. It is as meaningful as their sorting red and blue circles and squares, and it may make more sense later on.

Visit places where recycling classification activities go on: trash depots, bottle depots, receiving rooms of Goodwill Industries or Salvation Army stores. Visit neighborhood cooperative goods exchanges or secondhand services. Take children to a household auction. If you do not have services which recycle clothing, household goods, furnishings, and tools, maybe families of your center or neighborhood would like to start one.

105
YOUNG
CHILDREN
AND THE
ENVIRONMENT:
CYCLES

Reusables from home can serve as play materials, storage containers, for drama, water play, and creative activities, and as science experiments.

Ask children to bring reusables from home: rags, plastic containers, egg cartons, old magazines, etc. You and children can find uses for them as play materials, storage containers, for drama, water play, and creative activities, and as science experiments. You will find meat, milk, juice, cottage cheese, and oleomargarine containers useful. Use paper rolls, cardboard boxes, paper packaging and inserts.

Use fabric scraps and worn clothing creatively. Make collages, patchwork bags and backpacks for you and children. Do things with strips of cloth: braided rugs and chairseats, weaving, and crocheting. Children who learn to tie shoes can also learn to tie knots in cloth strips—macrame. Strips of cloth are handy ties for everything—try them as substitutes for tape or gift ribbon.

Find a source of paper that has been used on one side. Children will know what to do with the other side. Almost any office has such paper that is "waste," and computers produce an incredible amount.

Wipe and reuse aluminum foil if you can. Recycle it when no longer useful.

Take your own used paper bags—or a shopping bag you have made of scraps of material—when taking children shopping.

Try to find outlets for goods and food beyond your needs. Children may be able to save plate scraps for someone's chickens or goats, for example.

Make a compost pile for your garden. This consists of layers of grass clippings, leaves, or weeds layered with soil and with vegetable and fruit scraps, peelings, and wastes, as well as pet manure, the dumpings from your gerbil cage, and an occasional eggshell. Compost can be piled in a fenced enclosure away from play areas or kept in a barrel. It should be kept covered with a plastic sheet during fly season or in dry weather. Compost has to "cure" for several months—change needs time. Older children will take great interest in this organic decomposition part of the vegetation cycle. It is a good way for them to appreciate that organic material returns to the earth to renew it for new productivity, completing the circular cycle.

Teach a reverence for decomposers. Bacteria, molds, fungi, mushrooms, and some other plants are natural recyclers. They are the forms of life which break down and use "wastes," or materials other forms of life discard. Some make nutrients which enrich the soil without harming the waterways.

Teach a respect for animal and human feces. Manure, bowel movements, animal deposits—by whatever culturally appropriate terms parents and teachers wish to call them—are an essential part of health and of life's food cycles. They are a part of food chains for decomposers. They are an organic resource our society has been slow to acknowledge. Children should learn these substances are much more significant to life than they are sources of bathroom humor. The value of manure and dead animal materials as soil enrichment has been known for centuries in many cultures with successful, healthy patterns of living. If properly recycled, manure can increase food productivity and maintain natural balances. Children can at least learn it has value.

Balance Is Beautiful

The aesthetic value of a harmonious relationship seems universally pleasing to humans. We like systems which work smoothly and well. We find joy in calmness, in a good match, or in equilibrium. Balance is important. Children learn of balance as they pull to a stand and start to walk. They experiment with weight distribution and compensation as they sway back and forth to keep standing. Natural systems work in much the same way.

Pollution is a substance out of place and out of control. Pollution means substantial imbalance. All forms of life suffer in a polluted system. Because of earlier education efforts and publicity, many elementary children use "litter" or "pollution" as catchall terms for all of the environmental evils they know. Certainly the current supplies of air, water, food, and land are crowded with substances, sounds, and temperatures which do not belong there. As I pointed out in Chapter Three, there are many hazards in children's environments. Some of them are unnatural, put there by humans. Children can learn to protect themselves to some extent. In doing so, they are also learning about pollution and balance. Here are a few activities which focus on pollution and its avoidance or correction.

107
YOUNG
CHILDREN
AND THE
ENVIRONMENT:
BALANCE
IS BEAUTIFUL

Wash all commercial nonpackaged food thoroughly, especially fruits and vegetables. Most of these crops are grown with chemicals added. Pesticides are substances which poison pests, usually insects. Herbicides are chemicals which kill weeds and discourage undesirable plant growth. We should show sensible caution with *anything* which destroys any form of life. We should question the effects of any such product on other forms of life, especially young life.

Observe with children any sources of air pollution in your area. Watch heavy exhaust from an automobile—especially if you can see it condense and spatter on the snow or under the bumper, but keep children away from the source. If you have a view of your city or neighborhood, notice dark, smoky areas of air. Can you trace the sources? Do some chemicals and gases in the air hurt your nose or eyes? That's pollution.

Wipe the leaves of a tree or a shrub in a parking lot or near a busy street with a white tissue or cloth. Compare this to wiped leaves of the same kind of tree growing in an area away from traffic. If pollution is heavy in one area, you will find noticeable differences.

In a city, take children to watch an old building or monument being sandblasted. Or sandpaper a small section of the stone trim of an old building near a busy street. The accumulation of carbon compounds from the air can be astounding. It is soot, oil, and other pollutants, not "dirt" or soil.

Teach children about diseases and air pollution. We teach children in many ways that diseases come from microorganisms. We indict "germs"; we have people use only their own cups and toothbrushes; we dispose of nose tissues; we cover sneezes and coughs; we teach in so many ways that respiratory diseases are airborne. Good. Now, how about the diseases and conditions strongly associated with air pollution? They are many and deadly. We know about lung cancer, pulmonary emphysema, bronchial asthma, and chronic bronchitis—not to mention dizziness, headaches, eye irritations, blurred vision, delayed reflexes, eczema, stomach cancer, infant mortality, and disruption of normal child development (Pavoni et al. 1974). It seems reason enough to do something about air pollution, too. "Given the appropriate economic stimulus, there are no obvious technological difficulties involved in solving any pollution problem" (Boughey 1971, p. 366). There are things you can do in addition to group actions and political pressures.

Strongly discourage smoking in your children's center at all *times.* Smoking pollutes air. Furthermore, "As a result of animal experiments, it is suspected that pollutants act synergistically, that inhaling a mixture of two pollutants will have five or six times the effect of inhaling either one singly" (Boughey 1971, p. 329). This means if adults smoke in environments which are already somewhat polluted by wastes, the combination is much worse than either pollutant alone, or than just adding.

Anytime you are doing a filtering, sieving, or taking-apart activity, children can also be aware of pollutants, substances which do not belong. Filters on exhaust fans or unrolled filter cigarette butts tell the tale.

Children can learn the difference between steam or fog and air which is thick with solid particles, smoke, and other pollutants. Fog and steam revert to water; they will leave a filter wet but clean. Polluted air can be filtered but leaves black or brown or yellowish solids. Filtering is only one solution to the problem but one children can understand. If you know persons who wear air masks, that is a type of filter too.

As children learn what dissolving means, they can also realize many products do not dissolve, *or do not dissolve completely.* High use of paper products can pollute waterways and the ocean, as well as clog sewer lines. Help children pour a liter of water through a sieve. Soak a large wad of toilet paper in the water for a day or two. Pour the water through a sieve again. You will begin to see what is happening to the offshore ocean waters. Try it with other kinds of paper.

Encourage children to experiment and compare. What will happen to six open jars of water on the windowsill if children add a small amount of soil to one, scrape a plate of food scraps into one, put a wad of newspaper into one, mix detergents into one, add a little bit of all these substances into one, and leave one alone. You could help children remember to observe—look at *and* smell—their concoctions every day. These are the same things which go into water sewage systems. Which one would you pour into your fish tank?

Children need to observe and know that oil and water do not mix. If you are walking along almost any shoreline with children, you may have a chance to observe oil, scum, fatty chunks of garbage or sewage, or foam from detergents. In the city, walk with children around a parking lot after a rain. Note the oil spills, water runoff from the oily surfaces, and gasoline "rainbows" in the puddles.

Some materials give off color in water, some do not. Some colors are "fast," meaning they have become so strongly fixed into the fabric, paper, food, or whatever they are coloring, that they do not dissolve or fade in water. Children can experiment with a red cotton knit, a piece of real indigo blue denim, polyester fabrics, etc. Soak some crepe paper, boil some color-added hot dogs. Some dye chemicals are harmless, but some are poisonous. At this writing, the controversy over Red Dye No. 2 still rages. It has been used in many foods but appears to present serious health risks.

Right now research is underway to assess the wisdom of burning large amounts of paper which contains cadmium yellow, the bright yellow dye in paper stock and printers' ink. Children can and should use colors and learn about colors by mixing their own paints and food colorings. They should also be aware that eating, sucking on, etc., colored paper could be dangerous. Research on the effects of artificial color and other additives to children's foods has already raised serious questions, especially in relation to the dramatic increase in hyperactivity conditions in children. Boughey pointed out in 1971 there were one-half million different food additives. You should watch for reports of research findings concerning additives. Meanwhile, help children understand additives and compounds and colors.

109
YOUNG
CHILDREN
AND THE
ENVIRONMENT:
BALANCE
IS BEAUTIFUL

Even very young children understand picking up litter. Children can be encouraged to take two bags on their walk or field trip, one for treasures and one for trash. Cleanup activities of any sort have an environmental rationale. Help children understand it. They should also learn the need to wash their hands after handling polluted material.

Noise is a pollutant. "Unlike air, water, and land pollutants, noise is not tangible. It is a waste product which occurs only as excess energy in the air" (Pavoni et al. 1974, p. 212). Excessive noise can, however, cause hearing impairment and loss. It can damage the ears of humans and other animals. It appears to affect sleep patterns and body processes. It increases psychological tension, promotes fatigue, and interferes with performance of mental tasks. Children have ended up on the defensive about noise; they may have the idea that their own noise is a major source of adult irritation. Actually, it is not high on the list—compared to jackhammers or jet airplanes. Children need to know more about sounds in order to understand noise, which is unwanted sound. Some suggested activities are:

- Help children make tape-recordings of sounds of their own choosing, indoors and outdoors. Problems of background noise and interference come up—that is good. Help children discover conditions necessary to do an effective recording. Help them analyze the components and levels of various contributors to the background noise. How does one find or create a quiet place? (That should be under survival skills!)

- Focus observations on various animal sounds. Focus on various animals' *responses* to various sounds. Do they raise their heads, turn, stay still, twitch ears or noses, make sounds which seem to be answering? Do certain sounds seem frightening? How do people listen? How do people respond to sounds?

- Encourage experimentation with sounds. Feel each other's throats while talking, singing, humming, shouting, laughing. Talk through short and long paper rolls. Make and use a megaphone. Listen to and examine various musical instruments. Try to help children figure out how they work. Beat drums; put paper clips, beads, or other small objects on the drum head and beat again. Blow up a balloon and release the air, pulling the opening into a slit, more tightly, then more loosely to vary the sound. When some child learns to whistle is a good time to think about whistles and whistling. Make whistles; examine various kinds of whistles to see how they work; listen to whistling animals and birds.

- You would not deliberately set up any situation to startle a child, of course. But it may happen that Jill slams a box of books down on a table and the sharp noise startles Joey. You have an opportunity to point out that humans react in a certain way to a noise they are not expecting. The whole body "jumps"—muscles tighten, breathing and heart rate increase. Some noise pollution is from such sharp, sudden sounds; these are the body stresses which result. Once you know what caused the noise, or hear it repeatedly, it no longer has that effect.

Overpopulation is another kind of imbalance. All forms of life are related; all contribute to the balance of the biological system of which they are a part. If one kind of life outdoes the others, it makes waves which can drown the system. Usually, natural processes bring things into balance again—one way or another. This may be what happens when children plant 385 carrot seeds in a one-pound plastic butter container. How many come up? How many can that amount of soil feed and support so they grow to be carrots? Planting varying numbers of seeds, beans, etc., and noting how many sprout, then how many seedlings mature, is a good population experiment for children. Observing how large plants, trees, and shrubs grow can be enlightening. Many seedlings start, but only a few trees grow in a small patch of ground. Rodent cannibalism is a harsh lesson, and not advised for young children. A large and increasing number of mice in a small cage will probably eat each other even though there is enough food available for all. This is a dramatic example of overpopulation stresses.

Older children are ardent census-takers when they learn to count. They can count the number of plants or insects of a specified type in a given area. Compare the number of dandelions in a square meter of vacant lot ground to the number in the sand area on the north side of the school building. Help children analyze the conditions for growth in two areas with very different population numbers.

Imbalance is ugly and frightening. We do not want children to be frightened, but vast numbers of adults who are scared could accomplish something. Fighting environmental disharmony—pollution, waste, overconsumption—is a most notable and neglected form of child advocacy. If we can fight this one successfully, all of our children may still have some choices when they grow up, choices they can make in good health.

Ecosystems

Balance *is* beautiful. When an ecosystem is harmonious, all forms of life flourish. An ecosystem is a community of living things interacting with each other and with their nonliving environment. An ecosystem includes energy, food, living organisms, and such factors as light/darkness, water/dryness, air, temperature, the swell of the land, or currents of water. It may be an ecosystem on or under the land, in the ocean, or in fresh water. You and children share one. You sometimes experience others: the park, the vacant lot, the downtown area, the suburbs, the farmer's fields, the mountains, the deserts, the forests, etc.

It would be logical to assume that the concept of ecosystem, with all of its intricate patterns and relations, would be a difficult one for children. It seems likely that thorough understanding of ecology (the study of ecosystems) and its methods requires maturity. However, young children, because of their own natural egocentrism, seem to presume the environment is there for the interacting. They begin to identify the significant eco-elements early in their lives. The importance of their daily food, sleep, and activity routines; their reliance on known persons, things, and places; their attentions to small details; and their knowledge of what is right and proper, like the sun being in the sky, suggest the world as they know it. These are all ecologically significant categories, too. Increasing the focus on interrelationships is part of the teaching job. We can also begin to emphasize the total concept of ecosystem, even though it, too, takes a long time to develop. It is another version of what we have called "a child's world."

One of the best ecology teaching devices is to help children recreate life conditions. You do this in many ways when you facilitate play. What would happen if there was no housekeeping area in your center and you said to the children, "We want to set up a place right in this space to be like a little house or apartment to play in. What will we need to put in here?" Or, what would happen if you placed only a small inventory of homemaking equipment in a pile and let the children set it up and let their activities and comments suggest additions? Or what if the children arrived at kindergarten on a particular morning and you said, "Look what I bought for us at the pet store. This beautiful lizard is called a chameleon." Then, after time for lots of turns and investigation, questions of habitat may arise. If they don't, you could say, "You know chameleons are desert animals. We are going to have to make ours a special place to live. How can we make a desert in Ames, Iowa?"

Or, what if a group of primary children have decided to do a Hansel and Gretel theme with puppets. First they need to fix the puppet theater set to depict a forest. What do you need for a forest? Or, what if someone gives your daughter a jar full of guppies for her birthday? How do you set up an aquarium, with children, so you all understand the essential elements and conditions for the fish to survive and thrive? Or, suppose at the day care center, children are playing in wet sand. "This is a big castle!" Mac announces. You might say, "Yes, that's a good job." If you want to stimulate further constructive planning on Mac's part, instead of asking if he can make it bigger, ask "Where is your castle located, Mac? What kind of place is around it?"

If we focus on ecosystems, on ecological thinking, on a world in balance, we will do some things differently. We will not do all of the arranging *for* the children; we will do some of it *with* them. Even the room arrangement has many aspects of ecological science. You have been waiting a long time to get a piece of carpeting. Now, can the children help figure out where to put it? Can they experiment dropping blocks on the bare floor, then on the carpet? Can they tape-record the two experiences and resample them?

We will place not only cars and trucks near the block area, but also small sets of community people, furniture, playground equipment, signs, streetlights, trees, grass, and other regulatory devices of community interaction. You can make sets of these by gluing magazine cutouts to cardboard—children can help. I remember, especially with older children, their joys in

111
YOUNG
CHILDREN
AND THE
ENVIRONMENT:
ECOSYSTEMS

How do you set up an aquarium, with children, so that you all understand the essential elements and conditions for the fish to survive and thrive?

recreating life scenes with miniatures—farm sets, gas stations, doll houses, railroad stations, and trains. Older children enjoy making dioramas, miniature scenes such as museums sometimes use.

Toddlers will not be interested in these elaborations in the name of ecology. But they will enjoy activities concerning things-in-their-appropriate-places; things-which-fit-in-a-certain-way; things-which-work; things-which-have-names; etc. These are ecology activities, too.

113
YOUNG
CHILDREN
AND THE
ENVIRONMENT:
ECOSYSTEMS

If you want to bring ecology to your center and your children, you will spend a lot of time with aquariums, terrariums, planters, and large animal cages which recreate some of the pets' native conditions. Any of these can be an ecosystem in and of itself. You may have the luxury of raising your gerbil colony in a big, deep sandbox, where these desert creatures can tunnel and house themselves in burrows and leap about with ease. You can buy, but also make, ant farms. Or try an earthworm farm, in a deep, large glass jar with heavy paper rolled inside, and the worms in their moist earth, around the area in between. You may need to raise mealworms for that chameleon (speaking of food chains), keeping them in moist vermiculite in a glass jar, plastic shelf box, or sheet cake pan with lid, air holes, and light source. Feed them cereal, unsugared and uncolored. Be sure to guide children to think about and help plan the combination of elements which make any of these systems work. (Some of these suggestions are from Meisels 1975.)

What if the systems do not work? If you water your cactus three times a day, it will die. If three children each water it once a day, it will die, too. You may learn the hard way that some conditions are very specific for living things. (I recently heard of a Vermont teacher who guided her third-graders to watch the newspapers for reports of the weather in Phoenix, Arizona. When it rained in Phoenix, the Vermont children watered their cactus.) If a plant or animal dies, we want to think about why. We want to help children learn from this experience and correct the conditions, if the conditions had anything to do with the death. Then try again. That would be important to the children, too. Growth is based on having another opportunity.

Virginia Lee Fisher has given us some ideas about ecology awareness, especially on the playground.

First—look at the play yard as an ecological environment. What does that mean? In an ecological system elements are interdependent, relate to and grow with each other. How does that relate to children and a play area? The people (children and adults), growing things, materials and objects are the elements. Interdependence, *for example, would include the tree that provides shade for the people and the people who see that the tree receives water for growth; the need to dig in the ground and the need of seeds to be planted in well loosened soil; or the preference to walk on grass instead of mud and simple care of grass to keep it alive.* Relating and interacting *could include bruising a toe when a rock is dropped (plus learning about gravity and weight); watching a small bud become a yellow flower (and learning about time and waiting); hearing the sound of wind in the pine trees; digging, planting a seed—then finally eating a radish; finding an earthworm, watching it wiggle and even finding it stops wiggling forever if it is left on a hot sidewalk; feeling the coldness of water and discovering the shape on which it is poured, and how it acts to change the shape of sand and soil (Carson 1965).* Relating *and interacting can include ignoring and destroying as well as caring and enjoying.*

Caring *and* enjoying *begin with knowing all elements of the ecological system. If the "ecology" is the play yard, then we must know the plants, materials and objects—their potentials and their purpose—just as we know the children. Adults are responsible for organizing the ecology so that children can be active and pursue their interests; so they can identify, use and help care for the elements in their environment as part of the play typical of children of a particular age. (Fisher, n.d.)*

5

BRINGING IT
TOGETHER

I began with the purpose of making us all more aware of the science around us and presenting ways in which teachers can guide science experiences in order to enhance children's learning. I have emphasized not only the nature of science, but also the science of nature. I have suggested concentration on experience with natural materials, many forms of life and their sustenance, and environmental dynamics. Young children, because of *their* natures, are significant activists in the education and learning processes which are also the processes of scientific method. Early childhood education is based on the science of human development. Since science forms a basis for this educational approach, and since development as we know it provides the rationale, science experiences of many kinds make congenial curriculum.

Children are important. Teachers are important. Science is important. The content of the science curriculum for early childhood centers and homes should be based on individual children themselves. The personal ecology of each child is *the* basic science from which all other science understandings grow. From each child's science with her or his environment will come the experiences which can accumulate as survival skills and as environmental awareness and responsibility.

I have discussed some teaching techniques or methods which can sponsor the processes of growth, development, and science learning all at the same time. Because science planning is often an area of curriculum that teachers bemoan, I suggest upending old practices in the name of new science for new children. There are ideas for you to change it, switch it around, do it differently, refresh it—or try it. The results for children, and potentially for yourself as well, will be worth the effort. Adults seem to be able to drop outmoded proprieties by the wayside and can also find ways to expand experience and knowledge, therefore comfort, as teachers. That way, "doing what is comfortable" for the teacher does not become a limitation on the growth of children's minds and bodies.

I have presented some community resource ideas and printed references and have also urged you to think about using many years of recorded scientific investigation, folklore, and the commonsense conclusions from the experiences of generations of mature, intelligent human beings all over the world and in many, many cultures, as a composite science. Let's draw on all of these for contemporary science experiences for children. Science is lore that is true, that is repeatable and reliable and reasonable, that works. Early childhood science can make the bonds between natural and vicarious experiences, too: between periwinkles and pictures, robins and records, bugs and books, sandhills and stories. Science can bring many kinds of experiences together.

Science experiences can add momentum to our goal of helping children understand, enjoy, and cope with their lives and their environments in the present and in the future. Science demonstrates the survival value and biological necessity of balance, harmony, interdependence, and cooperation among all the living inhabitants of the earth, both plant and animal—including human. Perhaps if human beings begin to learn this while they are very young, they will find that happiness, productive fulfillment, comfort, and survival are not mutually exclusive.

Science is a way of doing things and solving problems. It is a style which leads a person to wonder, to seek, to discover, to know, and then to wonder anew. It is a style in which good feelings of joy, excitement, and beauty accompany these active interactions with one's world. Not only children but adults can experience science. It is a way of life.

APPENDIX

Some Common Poisonous Plants*

Not every poisonous plant is included in this chart because the list is simply too long. There are at least 700 species of plants in the United States and Canada that are known to have caused death or illness.

Plant	Toxic Part	Symptoms and Comment
House Plants		
Calla	Rhizome	Burning mouth and throat, vomiting.
Castor bean	Seeds	Burning sensation in mouth and throat. Severe vomiting and diarrhea, convulsions, kidney damage. One or two beans are near the lethal dose for adults.
Cyclamen	Tuber	Poisonous.
Dieffenbachia (dumbcane), caladium, elephant's ear, some philodendrons	All parts	Severe burning of mucous membranes of mouth, tongue, lips, and throat, nausea, vomiting, diarrhea, salivation, rare direct systemic effects; speech may become unintelligible. Death has occurred when tissues at back of tongue are swelled and block air passage to throat. Sap from dieffenbachia is especially toxic to open cuts.
Rosary pea (jequirity bean, crabs-eye precatory bean)	Seeds	Among the most highly toxic of natural materials. Severe gastrointestinal irritation, incoordination, paralysis, abdominal pain, vomiting, severe diarrhea, cold sweats, drowsiness, weak pulse, circulatory collapse, coma, hemolytic anemia. Less than one seed, if thoroughly chewed, is enough to kill an adult.
Flower Garden Plants		
Aconite, monkshood	Roots, flowers, leaves, seeds	Restlessness, salivation, nausea, vomiting, vertigo. Although people have died after eating small amounts of garden aconite, poisoning from it is not common.

*Adapted from "A New Look at Poisonous Plants," *Family Safety Magazine*, National Safety Council; *Texas Day Care* 28 (March 1971): 9-12; "Please Don't Eat the Flowers," Georgia Department of Human Resources, Division of Physical Health; "Poisonous Plants" compiled by Guy L. Hartman, M.D.; and author's sources. The information contained in this chart has been compiled from sources believed to be reliable and to represent the best current opinion on the subject.

Plant	Toxic Part	Symptoms and Comment
Autumn crocus	All parts, especially bulbs	Burning pain in mouth, gastrointestinal irritation. Children have been poisoned by eating flowers.
Columbine	Berries	Poisonous.
Dutchman's breeches (bleeding heart)	All parts	No human poisonings or deaths, but a record of toxicity for livestock is warning that garden species may be dangerous.
Four o'clock	Roots, seeds	Poisonous.
Hyacinth, narcissus, daffodil	Bulbs	Digestive upset including nausea, vomiting, trembling, and diarrhea when eaten even in small amounts. May be fatal.
Foxglove	All parts, especially leaves, flowers, seeds	One of the sources of the drug digitalis. May cause dangerously irregular heartbeat, digestive upset, vomiting, diarrhea, abdominal pain, severe headache, tremors, and mental confusion. Convulsions and death are possible.
Iris	Underground rhizome, also developed leaves, fleshy portions, stem	Severe digestive upset from moderate amounts of cultivated or wild irises, vomiting and diarrhea. Juice causes blisters on lips and mouth.
Jonquil	Bulbs	Vomiting and diarrhea, trembling.
Larkspur, delphinium	All parts, especially seeds, young plant leaves	May be fatal. Burning sensation of mouth and skin, vomiting, low blood pressure, weak pulse, convulsions.
Lily-of-the-valley	All parts, especially leaves, flowers, fruit (red berries)	In moderate amounts can cause irregular heartbeat, digestive upset, vomiting, and mental confusion.
Nicotiana, wild and cultivated	Leaves	Nervous symptoms. Poisonous or lethal amounts can be obtained from ingestion of cured smoking or chewing tobacco, from foliage of field-grown tobacco or from foliage of garden variety (flowering tobacco or nicotiana).

Plant	Toxic Part	Symptoms and Comment
Pimpernel	All parts	Poisonous.
Pinks	Seeds	Poisonous.
Snow on the mountain	All parts, especially leaves, sap, honey made from nectar	Severe irritation of mouth, vomiting and diarrhea, dermatitis, blindness.
Spider lily	Bulbs	Poisonous.
Star of Bethlehem	Bulbs	Vomiting and nervous excitement.
Sweet pea	Seeds	Paralysis, weak pulse, shallow breathing, convulsions.
Tulip	Bulbs	Vomiting, diarrhea, central nervous system depression.

Vegetable Garden Plants

Plant	Toxic Part	Symptoms and Comment
Eggplant	All parts except fruit	Fever, flushing, dry mouth, dilatation of pupils.
Potato	Vines, sprouts (green parts), spoiled tubers	Death has occured from eating green parts. To prevent poisoning from sunburned tubers, green spots should be removed before cooking. Discard spoiled potatoes. Vomiting and diarrhea, headache, shock, circulatory and respiratory depression.
Rhubarb	Leaf blade	Several deaths from eating raw or cooked leaves. Abdominal pains, vomiting and diarrhea, burning of mouth, ulcers of mouth and esophagus, and convulsions a few hours after ingestion. Without treatment, death or permanent kidney damage may occur.
Sweet potato	Leaves and stems	Vomiting, diarrhea, cyanosis, labored respiration, convulsions.
Tomato	Leaves	Hemolysis, apathy, drowsiness, salivation, labored respiration, paralysis.

Plant	Toxic Part	Symptoms and Comment
Ornamental Plants		
Agave	Leaves	Hepatitis, jaundice, coma, death. Dermatitis, kidney damage.
Amaryllis	Bulbs	Vomiting, diarrhea, tremor, convulsions.
Atropa belladonna	All parts, especially black berries	Fever, rapid heartbeat, dilation of pupils, skin flushed, hot and dry. Three berries were fatal to one child.
Bird of paradise, poinciana	Seeds and pods	Vomiting, diarrhea, dizziness, drowsiness.
Box	Leaves, twigs	Vomiting, diarrhea, convulsions.
Camera (red sage)	Green berries	Fatal. Affects lungs, kidneys, heart, and nervous system.
Carolina jessamine, yellow jessamine, wild yellow jessamine	All parts, especially flowers, leaves	Vomiting and diarrhea, convulsions. Poisoned children who sucked nectar from flowers. May cause depression followed by death through respiratory failure. Honey from nectar also thought to have caused three deaths.
Common privet	Black or blue wax-coated berries, leaves	Causes gastric irritation and vomiting, diarrhea, headache, shock, circulatory and respiratory depression.
Christmas rose	Roots, sap, leaves	Vomiting, diarrhea, central nervous system depression.
Cone flower	All parts	Abdominal pain, incoordination, central nervous system symptoms.
Crown of thorns	Sap	Swelling of tongue, mouth, and throat; vomiting and diarrhea.
Daphne	All parts, especially berries (commonly red, but other colors in various species), bark	A few berries can cause burning or ulceration in digestive tract. Abdominal pain, vomiting, bloody diarrhea, weakness, convulsions. Death can result.
English ivy	Berries, leaves	Excitement, diarrhea, difficult breathing, and eventually coma. Death can result.
Golden chain (laburnum)	Seeds, pods, flowers	Excitement, intestinal irritation, severe nausea with convulsions and coma. May be fatal.

Plant	Toxic Part	Symptoms and Comment
Heath family (laurels, rhododendron, azaleas)	All parts	Causes salivation, nausea, vomiting, anorexia, weakness, difficult or labored respiration, ataxia, and depression. "Tea" made from two ounces of leaves produced human poisoning. May be fatal.
Jasmine	Berries	Fatal. Digestive disturbance and nervous symptoms.
Lantana	Unripe greenish-blue or black berries	Can be lethal to children through muscular weakness and circulatory collapse. Less severe cases experience gastrointestinal irritation, vomiting, and diarrhea.
Morning glory	Seeds	Nausea, hallucinations, psychotic reaction.
Oleander	All parts, especially leaves, branches, nectar of flowers	Extremely poisonous. Affects heart and digestive system. Vomiting, abdominal pain, dizziness, slow and irregular heartbeat, dilation of pupils, bloody diarrhea, respiratory paralysis. Has caused death, even from meat roasted on its branches. A few leaves can kill a human being.
Scotch broom	Seeds, leaves	Weak pulse, intestinal paralysis, weakness, low blood pressure.
Spanish bayonet	Roots	Poisonous.
Virginia creeper	Berries	Vomiting and diarrhea. Two deaths have been reported.
Water lily	All parts	Death reported in animals.
Wisteria	Seeds, pods	One or two seeds may cause mild to severe gastrointestinal disturbances requiring hospitalization. Severe vomiting and diarrhea, collapse. However, with treatment recovery occurs in 24 hours. No fatalities recorded.
Yew	All parts, especially berries, needles, bark, seeds	Ingestion of English or Japanese yew foliage may cause sudden death as alkaloid weakens and eventually stops heart. Vomiting and diarrhea, dilated pupils, muscular weakness, coma, convulsions. Small amounts may cause trembling and difficulty in breathing.

Plant	Toxic Part	Symptoms and Comment

Trees and Shrubs

Plant	Toxic Part	Symptoms and Comment
Apple, crabapple	Seeds	Rapid respiration, groping, convulsions, coma. If eaten in large quantity, can cause death. One man died after eating a cupful.
Apricot	Kernels	Rapid respiration, gasping, convulsions, coma.
Avocado	Leaves	Death reported in animals.
Black locust	Bark, foliage, young twigs, seeds, sprouts	Digestive upset, vomiting, weakness, depression have occurred from ingestion of the soft bark. Seeds may also be toxic to children.
Buckeye, horsechestnut	Sprouts, nuts, leaves, flowers	Digestive upset and nervous symptoms (confusion, etc.), muscular twitching, weakness, incoordination, dilation of pupils, vomiting and diarrhea, central nervous system depression. Has killed children.
Buckthorn	Leaves, berries	Severe diarrhea.
Cashew	Husk of nut	Irritant oil with effect like poison oak or ivy.
Chinaberry tree	Berries	Nausea, vomiting, excitement or depression, symptoms of suffocation if eaten in quantity. Loss of life to children has been reported.
Elderberry	All parts (except ripe berries and flowers), especially roots, stems	Rapid respiration, gasping, convulsions, coma. Children have been poisoned by eating roots or using pithy stems as blowguns. Berries are the least toxic part but may cause nausea if too many are eaten raw.
Hydrangea	Leaves, buds	Nausea, vomiting, diarrhea, gasping, rapid breathing.
Jatropha (purge nut, curcas bean, peregrina, psychic nut)	Seeds, oil	Nausea, violent vomiting, abdominal pain. Three seeds caused severe symptoms in one person. However, in others as many as fifty seeds have resulted in relatively mild symptoms.
Mango	Fruit skin, tree sap, flower pedicel	Vomiting and diarrhea, skin irritation.

Plant	Toxic Part	Symptoms and Comment
Mock orange	Fruit	Poisonous.
Nutmeg	Seeds	Hallucinations, abdominal pain, flushing, dry mouth, drowsiness, stupor.
Oaks	All parts	Eating large quantities of any raw part, including acorns, may cause slow damage to kidneys. However, a few acorns probably have little effect.
Peach	All parts (except fleshy fruit), especially seeds	Vomiting and diarrhea, gasping, coma.
Pencil tree	Milky sap	Skin irritation, blindness, vomiting and diarrhea.
Rattle box (legume family)	All parts	Poisonous.
Wild black cherry, chokecherries, cultivated cherry	Leaves, pits, twigs, bark, seeds	Poisoning and death have occurred in children who ate large amounts of berries without removing stones. Pits or seeds, foliage, and bark contain HCN (prussic acid or cyanide). Stupor, vocal cord paralysis, twitching, convulsions.
Yellow oleander (be-still tree)	All parts, especially kernels of the fruit	In Oahu, Hawaii, still rated as most frequent source of serious or lethal poisoning in humans. One or two fruits may be fatal. Symptoms similar to fatal digitalis poisoning.

Plants in Wooded Areas

Plant	Toxic Part	Symptoms and Comment
Baneberry (doll's-eyes)	Red or white berries, roots, foliage	Acute stomach cramps, headache, vomiting, dizziness, delirium. Fatal.
Jack-in-the-pulpit, skunk cabbage	All parts, especially roots	Contains small needlelike crystals of calcium oxalate that cause burning sensation and severe irritation in mucous membranes of mouth, throat, and tongue; throat swelling and inadequate ventilation may be fatal; severe vomiting and diarrhea. In some cases, there is loss of voice. The swollen, immobile tongue may interfere with swallowing and breathing.
Marsh marigold	All parts, especially seeds, roots	Burning sensation of mouth and skin, vomiting, convulsions.

Plant	Toxic Part	Symptoms and Comment
Mayapple (mandrake)	Roots, foliage, unripe fruit	Large doses may cause gastroenteritis and vomiting. Ripe fruit is least toxic part and has been eaten by children—occasionally bowel catharsis results.
Moonseed	Berries	Blue-purple color, resembling wild grapes. May be fatal.
Mushrooms (some varieties)	All parts	Abdominal cramps, thirst, lacrimation, salivation, labored breathing, vomiting and diarrhea, coma, convulsions.
Poison ivy	All parts	Irritation to skin; fatalities have resulted from eating leaves.
Poison oak	All parts	Irritation to skin.
Poison sumac	All parts	Irritation to skin.
Water hemlock (cowbane, snakeroot)	All parts, especially roots, young foliage	Salivation, tremors, delirium, violent convulsions, vomiting, diarrhea, respiratory depression. One mouthful of root may kill an adult. Many persons, especially children, have died after eating this plant. Roots are mistaken for wild parsnip or artichoke.

Plants in Fields

Plant	Toxic Part	Symptoms and Comment
Burning bush	Leaves	Poisonous.
Buttercup	All parts, especially leaves	Severe vomiting, diarrhea, muscular weakness, weak pulse, respiratory paralysis, convulsions. Irritant juices may injure the digestive system.
Corn lily	Foliage	Salivation, prostration, depressed heart action, hallucinations, headache, vomiting, and diarrhea.
Death camas	Bulbs	Depression, digestive upset, abdominal pain, vomiting, diarrhea. Fatal. One case of poisoning from flower reported.
Flax (linseed)	All parts, especially seeds	Rapid respiration, gasping, convulsions, coma.
Indian tobacco	All parts	Vomiting, weakness, stupor, contraction of pupils, coma.

Plant	Toxic Part	Symptoms and Comment
Jimsonweed (thornapple)	All parts, especially seeds and leaves	Thirst, hyperirritability of nervous system, disturbed vision, pupillary dilation, dry mouth, flushing, hallucinations, headache, nausea, high blood pressure, delirium. Four to five grams of crude leaf or seed approximates fatal dose for a child. Poisonings have occurred from sucking nectar from tube of flower or eating fruits containing poisonous seeds.
Lupine	Foliage and seeds	Labored breathing, depression, trembling, convulsions.
Marijuana	All parts, especially resin	Euphoria, increased sensitivity to stimulation, hallucinations, confusion, coma.
Milkweed	Sap	Poisonous.
Mustard	All parts, especially roots	Vomiting, diarrhea, kidney damage.
Nightshades, European bittersweet, horse nettle	All parts, especially unripe berry	Children have been poisoned by ingesting a moderate amount of unripe berries. Digestive upset, stupefication and loss of sensation, fever, rapid heartbeat, dilation of pupils, dry mouth, flushing. Death due to paralysis can occur. Ripe berries, however, are much less toxic.
Poison hemlock	All parts, especially roots, foliage, seeds	Root resembles wild carrot. Seeds have been mistaken for anise. Causes gradual weakening of muscular power and death from paralysis of lungs. Vomiting, diarrhea, convulsions.
Pokeweed (pigeonberry)	Roots, berries, foliage	Burning sensation in mouth and throat, digestive upset and cramps. Seeds thought to have caused one human fatality.
Tansy	Leaves and flower heads	Rapid and weak pulse, vomiting, convulsions.
Tobacco	All parts	Vomiting, diarrhea, slow pulse, dizziness, collapse, respiratory failure.

Christmas Plants

Plant	Toxic Part	Symptoms and Comment
Holly	Berries	No cases reported in North America, but thought that large quantities may cause digestive upset, vomiting, diarrhea, and central nervous system depression.
Jerusalem cherry	All parts, especially unripe fruit, leaves, flowers	No cases reported, but thought to cause vomiting and diarrhea, convulsions, respiratory and central nervous system depression.
Mistletoe	Berries	Can cause acute stomach and intestinal irritation, vomiting and diarrhea, cardiovascular collapse. Cattle have been killed by eating wild mistletoe. People have died from "tea" of berries. Both children and adults have died from eating berries.
Poinsettia	Leaves, flowers, sap	Can be irritating to mouth and stomach, sometimes causing vomiting and nausea, collapse, but usually produces no ill effects. Controversial. One death reported in 1919.

For further information consult:

Human Poisoning from Native and Cultivated Plants, by James Hardin and James Arena. rev. exp. ed. Durham, N.C.: Duke University Press, 1973.

Poisonous Plants of the United States and Canada, by John M. Kingsbury. 3rd ed. Englewood Cliffs, N.J.: Prentice-Hall, 1964.

BIBLIOGRAPHY

Association for Childhood Education International. "The Living World." *Childhood Education* 47, no. 4 (1971).

Association for Childhood Education International. "Outdoor Education." *Childhood Education* 44, no. 2 (1967).

Association for Childhood Education International. "The World's Bounty." *Childhood Education* 40, no. 8 (1964).

Austin Association for the Education of Young Children. "Ideas for Teaching with Nature." *The Idea Box*. Washington, D.C.: National Association for the Education of Young Children, 1973.

Baker, K. R. *Let's Play Outdoors*. Washington, D.C.: National Association for the Education of Young Children, 1966.

Behrens, J. *The True Book of Metric Measurement*. Chicago: Children's Press, 1975.

Bello, F. "The Young Scientists." In *The New Scientist*, edited by P. C. Ober and H. A. Estrin. New York: Doubleday-Anchor, 1962.

Bender, J. *Natural Materials–Tools for Learning*. Washington, D.C.: Association for Childhood Education International, 1969.

Boughey, A. S. *Man and the Environment*. New York: Macmillan, 1971.

Brenner, B. *Baltimore Orioles*. New York: Harper and Row, 1974.

Brenner, B. *Bodies*. New York: E. P. Dutton, 1973.

Brown, M. E. "Some Basic Equipment for Infant Classrooms." Boulder, Colo.: Mountain View Center for Environmental Education, University of Colorado, 1966.

Cailliet, G.; Setzer, P.; and Love, M. *Everyman's Guide to Ecological Living*. New York: Macmillan, 1971.

Caras, R. *A Zoo in Your Room*. New York: Harcourt Brace Jovanovich, 1975.

Carl, G. C. *Guide to Marine Life of British Columbia*. Victoria, B. C., Canada: British Columbia Provincial Museum, 1971.

Carmichael, V. *Science Experiences for Young Children*. Los Angeles: Southern California Association for the Education of Young Children, 1969.

Carson, R. *The Sense of Wonder*. New York: Harper & Row, 1965.

Cobb, V. *Science Experiments You Can Eat*. Philadelphia: J. B. Lippincott, 1972.

Cohen, D. *Night Animals*. New York: Julian Messner, 1970.

Colton, R. W., and Richtmyer, J. *Science Equipment in the Elementary School*.

Boulder, Colo.: Mountain View Center for Environmental Education, University of Colorado 1975.

Crase, D. R., and Jones, N. S. "Children Learn from Recycling." *Young Children* 29, no. 2 (January 1974): 79-82.

Dowden, A. O. *The Blossom on the Bough: A Book of Trees.* New York: Thomas Y. Crowell, 1975.

Elkind, D. *Children and Adolescents: Interpretive Essays on Jean Piaget.* New York: Oxford University Press, 1970.

Euston, C. *A Better Place to Be: A Guide to Environmental Learning in Your Classroom.* Washington, D.C.: U.S. Department of the Interior, 1974. (Order from: Superintendent of Documents, U.S. Government Printing Office, Washington, DC 20402. Stock No. 2400-00805, $1.25.)

Ferreira, N. "Teachers' Guide to Educational Cooking in the Nursery School—*An Everyday Affair.*" *Young Children* 29, no. 1 (November 1973): 23-32.

Finch, I. *Nature Study and Science.* London: Longman Group, 1971.

Fisher, V. L. "Ecology and Environments." Unpublished learning units. University of Missouri, 32 Stanley Hall, Columbia, MO 65201, n.d.

Gardner, D. B. "The Child as an Open System." In *Play: The Child Strives Toward Self-Realization,* edited by G. Engstrom, pp. 62-68. Washington, D.C.: National Association for the Education of Young Children, 1971.

Goldin, A. *Straight Hair, Curly Hair.* New York: Thomas Y. Crowell, 1966.

Gordon-Nourok, E. *The Magic of Science for Young Children.* San Rafael, Calif.: Academic Therapy Publications, 1975.

Hartsuch, P. J. *Think Metric Now!* New York: Penguin Books, 1974.

Hawkins, D. "Messing about in Science." *Science and Children* (February 1965): 5-9.

Hawkins, F. P. *The Logic of Action: Young Children at Work.* Boulder, Colo.: Mountain View Center for Environmental Education, University of Colorado, 1969; New York: Pantheon, 1974.

Hone, E. B.; Joseph, A.; and Victor, E. *A Sourcebook for Elementary Science.* New York: Harcourt, Brace, & World, 1971.

Hucklesby, S. "Opening Up the Classroom: A Walk Around the School." Urbana, Ill.: ERIC/ECE, 1971.

Isaacs, N. *Children's Ways of Knowing.* New York: Teachers College Press, 1974.

Kluge, J. "What the World Needs Now: Environmental Education for Young Children." *Young Children* 26, no. 5 (May 1971): 260-263.

Koocher, G. P. " 'Why Isn't the Gerbil Moving Anymore?': Discussing Death in the Classroom—and at Home." *Children Today* 4, no. 1 (1975): 18-21.

Lueck, P. E. "Planning an Outdoor Learning Environment." *Theory into Practice* 7, no. 2 (1973): 121-127.

Mayesky, M.; Neuman, D.; and Wlodkowski, R. J. *Creative Activities for Young Children.* Albany, N.Y.: Delmar, 1975.

McCall, R. B. "Exploratory Manipulation and Play in the Human Infant." *Monographs of the Society for Research in Child Development* 39, no. 2 (1974).

McGavack, J., Jr., and LaSalle, D.P. *Guppies, Bubbles, and Vibrating Objects.* New York: John Day, 1969.

McIntyre, M. "As Long as Three Brooms." *Science and Children* 13, no. 3 (1975a): 38.

McIntyre, M. "Research in Early Childhood." *Science and Children* 12, no. 4 (1975b): 30.

McIntyre, M. "Science Is Eating." *Science and Children* 12, no. 5 (1975c): 38.

McIntyre, M. "Taking an Insect View." *Science and Children* 13, no. 2 (1975d): 41-42.

Meisels, S. J. "Preschool Science Curriculum: Is It Art or Is It Science?" Paper presented at the National Association for the Education of Young Children Annual Conference, November 1975, Dallas, Tex.

National Science Teachers Association. *Metric Is Coming.* Washington, D.C.: National Science Teachers Association, 1973.

Neuman, D. "Sciencing for Young Children." In *Ideas That Work with Young Children,* edited by K. R. Baker, pp. 136-148. Washington, D.C.: National Association for the Education of Young Children, 1972.

Ovitt, J. "Foundations of Science." In *A Creative Guide for Preschool Teachers,* edited by J. Wylie, pp. 135-160. Evanston, Ill.: Western Publishing Co., 1966.

Pavoni, J. L.; Hagerty, D. J.; and Heer, J. E. *Preserving Man's Environment.* Louisville, Ky.: Data Courier, 1974.

Peterson, R. T. *A Field Guide to Western Birds.* Boston: Houghton Mifflin, 1961.

Piaget, J. *Biology and Knowledge.* Chicago: University of Chicago Press, 1971.

Pitts, M., ed. *Texas Day Care* (1971a) no. 28.

Pitts, M., ed. *Texas Day Care* (1971b) no. 30.

Pitts, M., ed. *Texas Day Care* (1975c) no. 42.

Pitts, M., ed. *Texas Day Care* (1975d) no. 43.

Remy, C. *Arm-in-Arm.* New York: Parents' Magazine Press, 1969.

Schmidt, V. T., and Rockcastle, V. N. *Teaching Science with Everyday Things.* New York: McGraw-Hill, 1968.

Schneider, H., and Schneider, N. *Science Fun with a Flashlight.* New York: McGraw-Hill, 1975.

Shugrue, S. K., ed. *Environmental Education in the Elementary School.* Washington, D.C.: National Science Teachers Association, 1972.

Shuttlesworth, D. E. *Animals That Frighten People.* New York: E. P. Dutton, 1973.

Shuttlesworth, D. E. *Gerbils and Other Small Pets.* New York: E. P. Dutton, 1970.

Sigel, I. "The Development of Classificatory Skills in Young Children: A Training Program." In *The Young Child: Reviews of Research, Vol. 2,* edited by W. W. Hartup, pp. 92-111. Washington, D.C.: National Association for the Education of Young Children, 1972.

Sigel, I. "Developmental Theory and Preschool Education: Issues, Problems and Implications." In *Early Childhood Education: The 71st Yearbook of the National Society for the Study of Education, Part II,* edited by I. J. Gordon, pp. 13-31. Chicago: University of Chicago Press, 1972.

Silverstein, A., and Silverstein, V. *Guinea Pigs: All about Them.* New York: Lothrop, Lee & Shepard, 1972.

Selected NAEYC Publications

Order from NAEYC
1834 Connecticut Avenue, N.W.
Washington, DC 20009

All prices include postage. For information about these and other NAEYC publications, write for a free publications brochure. Please enclose full payment for orders under $10.00.